THE YEAR YOU WERE BORN
1970

A fascinating book about the year 1970 with information on events of the year USA, births, sporting events, book publications, the cost of living, Oscar winners, book publications, movies, music, world events and adverts throughout the book.

INDEX

US EVENTS OF 1970

January

1 In Dallas, the University of Texas Longhorns, ranked #1 in the nation by the Associated Press, won the Cotton Bowl game, 21 to 17, in the final two minutes of their game against the #9 ranked Fighting Irish of the University of Notre Dame. The win allowed the Longhorns, already voted #1 in the final UPI poll, to stay unbeaten at with 11 wins and no losses or ties. The #2 ranked Penn State Nittany Lions also finished unbeaten, at 11-0-0, with a 10 to 6 victory in the Orange Bowl over the #6 University of Missouri Tigers.

2 California became the first of the 50 United States to permit "no-fault divorce", in which a divorce could be granted without the petitioner having to allege misconduct on the part of his or her spouse; other states would enact similar legislation, with dissolution of marriage being allowed simply on grounds of "irreconcilable differences" between the two partners. The Family Law Act applied to all pending divorce cases filed under the old law, as well as the new ones filed for dissolution, which became the preferred term. The law had gone into effect the day before, but courts were not open for proceedings on the holiday. On the first domestic court hearings in Los Angeles County on January 5, a record number of marriages were ordered ended in a single day, with the average time for a hearing being "less than two minutes per case".

3 At 8:14 p.m. local time, a large meteor entered the Earth's atmosphere over central Oklahoma and broke into fragments. The largest piece was a 22.6 pounds (10.3 kg) meteorite that was the first whose fall was captured on film by multiple camera stations. Four of the 16 stations in the Prairie Meteorite Network, operated by the Smithsonian Institution, had photographed the meteorite's descent. Using triangulation, astronomers at the Smithsonian Astrophysical Observatory determined that the object's impact had been near Lost City, Oklahoma. On January 9, using the coordinates from the observatory, the camera network's field manager, Gunther Schwartz, located the object on a snow-covered dirt road near Lost City.

4 In Houston, NASA's Deputy Chief George M. Low announced a revision in the Apollo moon exploration schedule, and the cancellation of the Apollo 20 lunar landing that would have taken place in 1975 at the Tycho crater. Low said instead that Apollo 13, 14, 15 and 16 would land before the end of 1971; that the Apollo program would be paused for the launch of the Skylab space station in July 1972, and subsequent missions to Skylab running through March 1973; and that Apollo 17, 18 and 19, with longer stays on the Moon, would take place in 1973 and 1974. According to the original NASA schedule for future launches, Apollo 20 would have been launched in December 1972 and would have landed at the Copernicus crater with astronauts Don Lind, Jack Lousma and Stuart Roosa. Roosa would later pilot the Apollo 14 mission and walk on the Moon, Lousma would pilot the Skylab 3 mission, and Lind would be a mission specialist on a 1985 flight of space shuttle Challenger. Apollo 19 was rescheduled by Low for December 1973, but would be canceled by NASA on September 2. Eventually, Apollo 17, the final manned lunar landing, would be launched on December 7, 1972.

7 A controversial episode on the CBS police drama Hawaii Five-O was broadcast for the first, and only, time. Titled, "Bored, She Hung Herself", the evening's offering was about a girl who was believed to have hanged herself but, "was she under the diabolic influence of her mystic boyfriends— or was it murder?" The theme of erotic asphyxiation was described for the first time on television. After a viewer "died trying the same technique", the show was never rebroadcast and would be omitted from the syndicated reruns of the popular series. In 2007, Paramount Home Video would release a set of DVDs packaged as "Hawaii Five-O: The Second Season", purposely omitting the word "complete".

January

10 The launch of the first insured American space rocket was aborted at the last moment after the countdown had reached zero. The successful launch of the Delta M booster rocket was covered by a casualty and liability insurance policy that would pay for damages if the rocket failed and damaged its payload, a commercial communications satellite. The event also marked the first time that a launch sequence was automatically shut down by a system on the rocket, rather than by the people at NASA ground control in Cape Kennedy. Although satellite insurance had been provided against damage to payloads for more than four years, the launch rockets themselves had never been covered. The Intelsat 3-6 was to be successfully launched five days later.

11 The last American Football League champions, the Kansas City Chiefs, upset the heavily-favored NFL champion Minnesota Vikings, 23-7, in Super Bowl IV.

14 With more than 20 suspected cases of typhoid fever among its passengers and crew, the luxury ocean liner SS Oronsay was placed under quarantine after arriving in Vancouver harbor, partway through its round-the-world cruise. Although 154 passengers Vancouver-bound passengers were allowed to leave for examination, the remaining 991 passengers and the 500 crew members were ordered to prohibit from disembarking until further notice. Most would spend the next three weeks on the ship while it sat at port. A spokesman for the Vancouver health department branded SS Oronsay "a floating bomb". The ship had departed London on December 16 for a four-month cruise and the disease was discovered after some of the crew were hospitalized in Los Angeles. In all, 70 people were hospitalized. About 700 passengers would be confined to the ship until it would finally sail out of Vancouver on February 4.

18 A full page advertisement in The New York Times was taken out by a group called "The Environmental Teach-In, Inc.", with the slogan "April 22. Earth Day." in preparation for the first United States nationwide event to call attention to the ecological crisis that was facing the world. "A disease has infected our country," the text said, "It has brought smog to Yosemite, dumped garbage in the Hudson, sprayed DDT in our food, and left our cities in decay. Its carrier is man." Seeking contributions for what has now become an annual event, the Environmental Teach-In went on to say "On April 22 we start to reclaim the environment we have wrecked."

20 The Super Fight, a simulated boxing bout between Muhammad Ali and the late Rocky Marciano, was shown on pay-per-view in 1,000 movie theaters in North America and around the world. The likely result, of the hypothetical fight between the two former world heavyweight boxing champions, was determined by data inputted to a computer, and enhanced by clips of possible outcomes that the two boxers had filmed during the summer before Marciano's 1969 death in a plane crash. Marciano and Ali (still referred to by the press as Cassius Clay) were, at the time, the only two title holders who had never been defeated. People, who paid five dollars apiece, for a ticket to the film, saw an ending where Marciano "floored Clay for the third time with a solid left hook" and in which "the taller, younger Clay was counted out in the 13th round."

22 The first scheduled airline flight for the Boeing 747 "jumbo jet", operated by Pan American Airways, departed from New York's John F. Kennedy International Airport at 1:52 in the morning local time (0652 UTC), after a delay of almost seven hours. Pan American Flight 001 was to have started its maiden flight at 7:00 the previous evening. Once aloft, the gigantic airplane carried 332 passengers and a Pan Am crew of 18 to London's Heathrow Airport, where it arrived at 1:05 in the afternoon (1305 UTC) Though the flight had been sold as a round trip, 128 passengers canceled their reservations to return to New York on the 747, "perhaps the greatest number ever compiled by a single airliner."

January

27 | A hoax perpetrated by a man who claimed that he had seen "Bigfoot" (also called "Sasquatch") caused a rush of more than 50 American and Canadian bounty hunters to Colville, Washington in search of the legendary creature. Joe Metlow, a mining prospector, announced that he had seen the 9 feet (2.7 m) tall beast, estimated to weigh 1,000 pounds (450 kg) in northern Stevens County, and offered to divulge the location of the sighting in return for a "suitable" payment. By January 30, the hunters searched Stevens County by airplane, by helicopter, and on foot. Metlow rejected all offers of payment (including one for $55,000) as unsuitable, and the Bigfoot hunters gave up after a few days of fruitless searching.

February

2 | U.S. President Richard M. Nixon sent the annual government budget proposal to Congress, sharply curtailing the American manned space program and raising the amount to be spent for welfare programs. The amount of money budgeted to government programs for the 1971 fiscal year was a little more than 200 billion dollars USD. Fifty years later, the budget for FY 2020 would be 23 times higher, at 4,700 billion dollars ($4.7 trillion).

3 | NASA made its second, and more successful launch of a rocket with electrostatic ion thrusters, as it put the SERT-2 probe into a polar orbit around the Earth The SERT-2 was sent up from Vandenberg Air Force Base in California at 6:50 in the evening local time. On July 20, 1964, the first SERT (an acronym for Space Electric Rocket Test) operated for 31 minutes. SERT-2 remained in orbit for more than 11 years, and its two mercury engine thrusters successfully operated for 3,781 hours and 2,011 hours (157 days and 84 days).

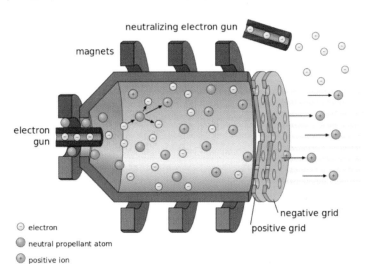

7 | Professional golfer Doug Sanders was struck on the head with a golf ball during the Bob Hope Desert Classic in Palm Springs, California, after being hit by an errant shot made by U.S. Vice President Spiro Agnew. Sanders had won the Desert Classic during the PGA Tour in 1966 and had been grouped with three celebrities, Agnew, Bob Hope and former movie star and U.S. Senator, George Murphy. Bruce Devlin of Australia would go on to win the PGA event.

16 | In a professional bout to determine the undisputed heavyweight boxing champion of the world, World Boxing Council champion Joe Frazier knocked out Jimmy Ellis, holder of the World Boxing Association, in the fifth round of a fight at Madison Square Garden in New York.

20 After the first mission of the supersonic D-21 TAGBOARD drone failed on November 10, the U.S. Central Intelligence Agency (CIA) made improvements to the computer software of its inertial navigation system, and "flew a completely successful test mission to validate the software" and a new "'fail-safe' feature" to allow "positive control of the drone's flight path" on aerial reconnaissance missions.

24 Joseph Franklin Sills, a 49 year old convicted robber in Texas, became the first person in the United States to be sentenced to 1,000 years in prison. A jury in Dallas had recommended the sentence after convicting Sills for the armed robbery of $73.10 from a Dallas dry cleaner, and meted out the punishment after being told that he had 20 prior felony convictions. Other juries in Texas would follow in recommending similarly long imprisonment time, primarily as a protest against Texas law, which allowed convicts to be eligible for parole after 20 years or after one-third of their sentence, had been served, whichever came first. Mr. Sills's sentence would be upheld on appeal.

25 A routine in an episode of the children's TV series Sesame Street was performed for the first time and would soon become a best-selling record, as the Muppet character Ernie sang "Rubber Duckie" (with Jim Henson supplying the voice) as an ode to the rubber duck bathtub toy. The latex toy duck had been invented by sculptor Peter Ganine, who applied for a patent on December 29, 1947 and received U.S. Patent No. 153,514 on April 26, 1949. The song itself was written by Jeff Moss and arranged by Joe Raposo.

28 The first-ever theft of lunar soil was carried out at the banquet hall of the upscale Bullocks Wilshire store in Los Angeles, where it had been on display for 300 guests attending a fundraising dinner. The 2.3 grams (0.081 oz.) sample, part of Moon Rock No. 50 brought back by the Apollo 11 astronauts, was unguarded and the display of the rock had not been authorized by NASA. The lunar sample had been on loan to the UCLA Institute of Geophysics and Planetary Physics since November. The LAPD recovered the purloined vial of dust two days later after receiving an anonymous phone tip that it had been dropped into a mailbox.

March

2   Burlington Northern Railroad, the longest railway in the world by number of miles served, was created by the merger of four railroads in the northern United States. The U.S. Supreme Court had upheld the merger on February 2, combining the Burlington Route (officially, the Chicago, Burlington and Quincy Railroad), the Great Northern Railway, the Northern Pacific Railway, and the Spokane, Portland and Seattle Railway into one network of 24,398 miles (39,265 km) of track in 18 U.S. states and two Canadian provinces. With combined assets of $2.8 billion USD, Burlington Northern was less than half as large as the Penn Central railroad's $6.5 billion properties.

6   Three members of the Weathermen, an American terrorist group, were killed in New York City when a pipe bomb they had constructed exploded prematurely. The group had settled in a four-story townhouse at 18 West 11th Street in Greenwich Village and was constructing explosives in the basement. Shortly before noon, dynamite in one of the bombs exploded and triggered secondary gas line blasts. Diana Oughton and Terry Robbins, who were working on a bomb, were killed instantly, along with Ted Gold, who had walked in to the home moments before the explosion. Cathlyn Platt Wilkerson, whose father owned the townhouse and was out of town, escaped along with another accomplice, Kathy Boudin. Another member of Weather Underground, Mark Rudd, would write later that the group had planned to place the bomb at a dance hall at Fort Dix, New Jersey, where U.S. servicemen and their dates would have attended a dance. Wilkerson would surrender to the police in 1980, and would spend 11 months in prison. Boudin would be arrested in 1981 after driving the getaway vehicle in an armored car robbery, remaining incarcerated until 2003.

11   Hawaii became the first state in the United States to allow abortion at the request of the woman, on the condition that the fetus not be viable outside the uterus and that the woman had been a resident of the state for at least 90 days. The bill had passed the state House of Representatives, 31-20, on February 18 and the state Senate followed, 15-9, on February 24. Personally opposed to abortion, Hawaii Governor John A. Burns refused to sign it into law, but also declined to veto the bill, allowing it to become law. Almost 1,200 abortions were legally performed in the first four months after the law took effect.

14   The U.S. merchant vessel SS Columbia Eagle was seized by two members of the crew in a mutiny while transporting bombs to the Thailand port of Sattahip. Armed with pistols, Clyde McKay Jr. and Alvin Glatkowski threatened the captain and the rest of the crew of the ship by claiming that they were prepared to detonate one of the bombs in the cargo. Twenty-four men evacuated in lifeboats and McKay and Glatkowski then forced the remaining 13 crew to pilot the vessel to Cambodia. The new government of Cambodia permitted Columbia eagle to leave on April 8, and imprisoned McKay and Glatkowski for extradition to the United States.

17   The United States Army charged 14 of its officers (including two generals) with suppressing information about the 1968 My Lai Massacre in South Vietnam, and referred charges for court martial. Charges would later be dropped against Major General Samuel W. Koster (who would be demoted to the rank of brigadier general) and against Brigadier General George H. Young, Jr.; Colonel Oran Henderson would be tried and acquitted reassigned after a court-martial. Lieutenant William L. Calley Jr. would be the only one of the officers to be tried and convicted.

22   The United States first used the BLU-82 bomb in combat, dropping the most powerful conventional weapon up to that time on North Vietnamese Army and Pathet Lao guerrilla troops in Long Tieng in Laos. The 15,000 pounds (6,800 kg) bomb, nicknamed the "Daisy Cutter", had originally been designed to clear jungles to create landing zones for helicopters because it could clear an area within a radius of 300 feet (91 m) without leaving a bomb crater.

23 U.S. President Nixon declared the nationwide walkout of postal workers to be a national emergency, and ordered the first of 2,500 United States troops to being sorting and moving six days' worth of undelivered mail. Busloads U.S. Air Force members arrived in New York City and began work that evening in the General Post Office in Manhattan, a second office serving the Wall Street financial district, and the main subdivision serving Brooklyn. The U.S. Department of Defense announced that 30,000 members of the Air Force, Army and Navy had been placed on alert, and called 12,000 from the 42nd Infantry Division of the multi-state U.S. Army National Guard to active duty, along with 15,000 reservists. At the peak of the strike, 627 American post offices had had work stoppages.

24 Buddy Baker became the first stock car racing driver to drive faster than 200 miles per hour on a race course. Baker was preparing for NASCAR's inaugural Alabama 500 race at Talladega when he drove a lap on the 2.66 miles (4.28 km) track in less than 48 seconds, averaging 200.447 miles per hour (322.588 km/h).

25 The first strike by post office workers in U.S. history came to an end, two days after President Nixon had called out the nation's military forces to sort and deliver the mail. During the eight day strike, 35,000,000 packages, letters and postcards had accumulated in New York City alone.

30 The American soap opera Somerset premiered on NBC as a spin-off of the more popular daytime serial, Another World. The new show was originally called "Another World in Somerset", while the parent show was renamed "Another World in Bay City". On the same day, the ABC network premiered two of its own soap operas, the short-lived The Best of Everything and A World Apart.

31 After 12 years in orbit, Explorer I, the first American satellite, reentered the Earth's atmosphere and burned up during its plunge to earth. Launched on January 31, 1958, Explorer I made 58,376 revolutions around the Earth before re-entering the atmosphere over the South Pacific Ocean at 11:47 UTC.

April

1   U.S. President Richard M. Nixon signed the Public Health Cigarette Smoking Act into law, banning cigarette television and radio advertisements in the United States effective January 2, 1971. The "one, big last day" on January 1 was permitted by Congress to allow television networks to get tobacco revenue for the college football bowl games on New Year's Day.

5   In the worst killing in California police history, four California Highway Patrol officers were shot and killed while confronting two armed suspects outside of a restaurant in Newhall, California. Officers Walt Frago, Roger Gore, George Alleyn, and James Pence were all fatally wounded within four minutes before midnight after Frago and Gore had stopped a car driven by Bobby Davis a passenger in the car, Jack Twinning, fired the first shots after Frago made his approach to the vehicle, and Gore was killed by Davis. The next day, Twinning killed himself after being cornered by police. Davis was arrested, and eventually hanged himself in prison, 39 years after the killings.

7   The Academy Awards were presented, and Midnight Cowboy became the first (and to date, the only) X-rated film to receive the Oscar for Best Picture and its director John Schlesinger was voted the award for Best Director. Screen legend John Wayne received his first and only Oscar for Best Actor, for his performance as Rooster Cogburn in the Western True Grit.

11   Apollo 13, carrying astronauts Jim Lovell, Fred Haise and Jack Swigert, was launched from Cape Kennedy at 2:13 in the afternoon local time (19:13 UTC), with plans to make the third manned landing on the Moon, and what would have been the first to explore the lunar highlands.

| **Jim Lovell** | **Fred Haise** | **Jack Swigert** |

12   The 1970 Alabama 500 was a NASCAR Grand National Series (now Monster Energy NASCAR Cup Series) event that was held on April 12, 1970, at Alabama International Motor Speedway (now Talladega Superspeedway) in Talladega, Alabama. As the inaugural running of what is now known as the GEICO 500, it helped to serve as a prime example of Talladega races yet to come.

Nord Krauskopf's Bobby Isaac won the pole position, and the race was won by Petty Enterprise's Pete Hamilton.

April

13 At 9:08 in the evening Central Time (April 14 03:08 UTC), the Mission Control team at the Manned Spacecraft Center in Houston, Texas, received word from the Apollo 13 crew that an oxygen tank in the command module had exploded, and that electrical power was gradually dropping, an event that led to an abort of the planned lunar landing. The mission shifted to recalculation of the Apollo 13 route in hopes of getting the three astronauts safely back to Earth. Nine minutes after the crew had finished a 40-minute live broadcast to television viewers, astronaut Fred Haise began alerting with the words "Okay, Houston..." and Jim Lovell followed with "I believe we've had a problem here." When ground control asked him to repeat the statement, Lovell said, "Houston, we've had a problem." Twenty-five years later, the film Apollo 13 would have actor Tom Hanks, as Lovell, saying "Houston, we have a problem." The initial observation was an under voltage in two of the power-producing cells. After 93 minutes, Haise reported that oxygen pressure in the command module was dropping, and by 10:59 p.m., Mission Control determined that the three LM fuel cells had failed, that only 15 minutes of electrical power remained, and that the crew should transfer immediately to the lunar module.

14 NASA canceled the scheduled landing of Apollo 13 on the Moon and began new calculations for a course that could swing the spacecraft around the Moon and then bring the command module and lunar module back to Earth. By 9:30 p.m. EST (0230 UTC 15 April), the ship had completed its circuit of the Moon and fired the engines to speed the spacecraft back toward the Earth.

15 At 00:21 UTC (7:21 p.m. April 14 Eastern time), the crew of Apollo 13 was partway through its "slingshot maneuver" around the far side of the Moon, at an altitude of approximately 158 miles (254 km) above the lunar surface. At that point, astronauts Fred Haise, Jack Swigert, and Jim Lovell had set a record for the furthest distance that human beings had ever traveled away from the Earth. During that time, they were 248,655 miles (400,171 km) above the Earth.

17 Apollo 13 splashed down safely in the South Pacific Ocean near American Samoa, and was recovered by the amphibious assault ship USS Iwo Jima. Astronauts Jim Lovell, Jack Swigert and Fred Haise reported that they were exhausted because the intense cold during the return trip had prevented them from sleeping.

18 The day after their safe return to Earth following a near disaster in space, the three Apollo 13 astronauts were presented the Presidential Medal of Freedom by U.S. President Nixon at a ceremony in Honolulu. Jim Lovell, Fred Haise and Jack Swigert were told by Nixon, "You did not reach the Moon but you reached the hearts of millions of people on Earth by what you did."

20 A new comic strip, Broom-Hilda, began its daily run in 69 American daily newspapers as one of the offerings of the Chicago Tribune Syndicate. Featuring a broom-riding witch as its title character, the strip is still drawn by cartoonist Russell Myers more than 49 years later. While Sunday, April 19, 1970, is sometimes listed as the date of the first strip, the appearance was limited to an advertisement in the Sunday comics section of the Chicago Tribune where Broom-Hilda told readers "My friends and I will be in the Tribune every day, starting tomorrow. Come and see us."

22 Earth Day was celebrated in the United States for the first time. The Associated Press reported the next day, "Across the nation, trash was gathered, streets swept, ponds and parks cleaned, trees and flowers planted" as "youth joined hands with age across the generation gap".

May

1 At 7:30 in the morning local time (0030 UTC) 8,000 United States Army troops followed South Vietnam's Army of the Republic of Vietnam (ARVN) troops into Cambodia's Kampong Cham Province, and expanding the American involvement in the Vietnam War to attack North Vietnamese Army (NVA) enclaves in an area known as the Fishhook. Helicopters and ground troops of the U.S. Army's 1st Air Cavalry Division and an ARVN airborne brigade caught the NVA off guard, while troops of the 25th Infantry Division drove their attack northward and westward; by May 3, the United States would claim 467 of the enemy had been killed, and only eight American soldiers Simultaneously with the invasion, U.S. President Richard Nixon was preparing to announce the invasion in a nationwide address, which began at 0200 UTC (9:00 in Washington, DC on Thursday night). Protests against the expansion of the Vietnam War began on American college campuses later in the day on Friday. For the first time in more than 50 years, the U.S. Senate Foreign Relations Committee voted to ask for a meeting with a U.S. President, after having been given no notice of the invasion, and the request was unanimous from both political parties.

6 The first wristwatch to use an LED display, the Pulsar watch, was introduced by the Hamilton Watch Company with a demonstration on The Tonight Show. After being told that the Pulsar's retail price was $1,500 (equivalent to $9,970 in 2019), Johnny Carson quipped, "The watch will tell you the exact moment you went bankrupt!"

8 The New York Knicks won their first National Basketball Association championship, defeating the Los Angeles Lakers, 113–99, in Game 7 of the championship series at New York's Madison Square Garden. Despite tearing a muscle in his thigh muscle four days earlier, Willis Reed chose to start the game for the Knicks and, with a shot of carbocaine and cortisone to help him endure severe pain, remained in until shortly before halftime, "inspiring his teammates merely with his presence on the court", and Walt Frazier scored 36 points. The Knicks led 69-42 at the half in a game which New York City residents could only watch on tape delay.

14 U.S. President Nixon signed a bill expanding the national school lunch program's coverage to 50% additional students, providing a free (or reduced price) lunch for schoolchildren whose family income was below the poverty line ($3,968 for a family of four in 1970). Lunch prices for eligible students could not exceed 20 cents (equivalent to $1.30 in 2019).

15 The 138th, and last, original episode of the TV spy spoof Get Smart was broadcast at 7:30 Eastern Time, bringing an end to the show after five seasons.

16 The first fatal injury ever sustained by a spectator at a Major League Baseball game occurred when a 14-year old fan, Alan Fish, was struck by a foul ball while at Dodger Stadium in Los Angeles. Alan Fish was sitting in the second row along the first base line and, in the third inning, a foul ball hit by Manny Mota struck him in the head. After getting treated at the stadium's first aid station, Fish returned to his seat to watch the remainder of the Dodgers' 5-4 loss to the Giants. As his headaches got worse, he was admitted to the children's hospital and lapsed into a coma the next day, and died four days after being struck.

25 The first sale of a programmable desktop computer was made when the Computer Terminal Corporation (CTC) sold 40 of its Datapoint 2200 computers to the General Mills Company of Minnesota. The original Datapoint had eight kilobytes (8K) of internal memory and its data could be stored on cassette tapes that could hold 130 KB capacity. Most of the machines were leased to buyers at a cost of $168 per month for each unit (equivalent to $1,100 per month in 2019), or sold for $1,280 ($8,500 equivalent) apiece.

May

30 Six people, all but one of them the occupants of a car that was "in the wrong place at the wrong time" were killed when a chartered Martin 4-0-4 airliner lost power shortly after takeoff from Atlanta's DeKalb–Peachtree Airport and crashed on to the east bound lanes of Interstate 285 east of the Moreland Avenue bridge. One passenger on the plane, which was transporting prospective home buyers from the Atlanta area to the Lehigh Acres Subdivision in Fort Myers, Florida, was killed. The dead in the car were a family of four two parents and two children, and another child who were on their way to a picnic. The accident was traced to the airport by a ground crew, who mistakenly filled the propeller plane's tanks with jet fuel.

June

3 U.S. President Richard M. Nixon announced in a nationwide television and radio address that American troops would be pulled back out of Cambodia after the achievement of "all our major military objectives", and that half of the 31,000 U.S. troops in Cambodia had been returned to fight in South.

4 The hijacking of a TWA Flight 486, and its 51 passengers, ended eight hours after it started, when police in at Dulles International Airport in Washington persuaded Arthur G. Barkley to leave the plane. Three hours earlier, Barkley had been paid the first ransom ever given to an American hijacker when TWA provided him with $100,750 when the Boeing 727 flight from Phoenix to Washington landed at its intended destination of Dulles. Barkley was upset, however, to discover that he was not being provided the ransom of $100,000,000 he had demanded and forced the plane to take flight again. Barkley would later be found not guilty by reason of insanity, of crimes arising from the wounding of Flight 486's pilot, and the air piracy charges would be dropped when he was committed to a hospital for the criminally insane.

11 Anna Mae Hays and Elizabeth P. Hoisington of the U.S. Army were formally promoted to the rank of brigadier general, making them the first female generals in American history. General Hayes was the director of the Army Nurse Corps, and General Hoisington commanded the Women's Army Corps.

Anna Mae Hays

Elizabeth P. Hoisington

12 Dock Ellis, a pitcher for baseball's Pittsburgh Pirates, threw the first no-hitter of the 1970 season while, he would claim later, he was high on the hallucinogenic drug LSD. In the 2 to 0 win in San Diego over the Padres, Ellis allowed eight walks On April 8, 1984, Ellis would claim that he had taken LSD six hours before the game because he hadn't realized that the Pirates were playing that day, let alone the starting pitcher. He said that he remembered little about the game other than a feeling of euphoria and that he was "zeroed in" on the catcher's glove.

13 "The Long and Winding Road" became the Beatles' 20th and final single to reach number one on the U.S. Billboard Hot 100 chart in the magazine's June 13 rankings. Billboard's magazine and Top 40 had been released on June 6. The song would stay a second week at #1 before dropping to #4 and moving back down the charts. During their six-year recording career, the Beatles had averaged a #1 hit single every 3.7 months.

15 The Land of Oz, an American theme park based on the Wizard of Oz book series and film, opened at Beech Mountain, North Carolina. It would suffer serious damage from a fire in 1975, and close in 1980, but still reopens periodically for special events.

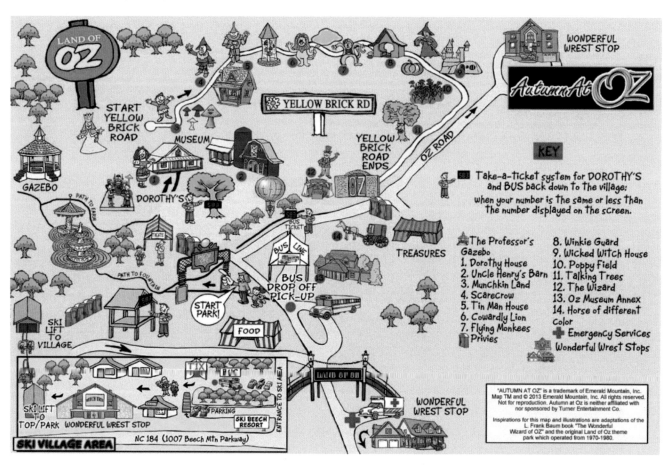

17 A bill to lower the voting age for Americans from 21 to 18 was passed Congress after the U.S. House of Representatives voted, 272 to 132, to join the U.S. Senate in amending the Voting Rights Act of 1965, effective January 1. Nixon signed the bill into law on June 22, but the relevant part of the amendment would be declared unconstitutional by the U.S. Supreme Court on December 21 in the case of Oregon v. Mitchell, in a finding that the federal government could only regulate national elections. The 26th Amendment to the U.S. Constitution would be ratified a little more than a year later in 1971 to lower the voting age in all elections.

June

21 In the largest U.S. corporate bankruptcy, up to that date, the Penn Central Railroad filed a petition for Section 77 bankruptcy. The board of directors of Penn Central voted to file the petition after the President Nixon withdrew a plan for a $200,000,000 guaranteed loan to the nation's largest railroad company in the face of opposition from Congress. U.S. District Judge William Kraft, Jr. signed the order on the petition at his Philadelphia home at 5:35 in the afternoon, allowing the petition but permitting Penn Central to continue operating its scheduled rail service until bankruptcy trustees could be appointed.

27 The International Football Association Board (IFAB) voted to change the rules of soccer football, and adopted the shoot-out as a method of determining a winner in a game where the score was tied at the end of regulation time and extra time. Under the adopted rule, each team would be allowed up to five kicks, similar to penalty kicks, and the team with the best of five tries would be awarded the victory.

29 In Jersey City, New Jersey, former world heavyweight boxing champion Sonny Liston came back from a defeat and defeated Chuck Wepner when the referee stopped the bout because Wepner was severely bleeding. The victory would prove to be Liston's last fight, and he was found dead in his home a little more than six months later. Wepner, nicknamed "The Bayonne Bleeder" for his hometown of Bayonne, New Jersey and his determination to keep fighting even after being cut, required more than 100 stitches to his face, and would later lose in a memorable bout in 1974 with world heavyweight boxing champion Muhammad Ali.

July

4 The radio music countdown show American Top 40 made its debut, with Casey Kasem as host, playing the most recent list of Top 40 most popular songs as ranked by Billboard magazine for the preceding week. Initially, only 10 radio stations carried the syndicated program. The first song introduced (the #40 seller for the week) was Marvin Gaye's recording of "The End of Our Road", and the first number one hit was "Mama Told Me Not to Come" by Three Dog Night.

8 Twenty-five American judges agreed to spend a night in the Nevada State Prison in Carson City under the same conditions as the inmates, in the first experiment of its kind. The activity was sponsored by the University of Nevada, Reno, through a seminar of the National College of State Trial Judges (now the National Judicial College. Most of the judges shared a cell with minimum security prisoners, while some were placed in "the hole" (a holding cell) in solitary confinement. Upon walking out of the penitentiary the next day, the judges were in agreement that the conditions in U.S. prisons were shocking, and that prison reform was necessary.

11 An Athena V-123-D missile, launched by the U.S. Air Force, veered off course from the Green River Launch Complex in Utah, and impacted 180 miles (290 km) south of the border between the U.S. and Mexico. Although the missile was reported in the press release to be unarmed, it was actually a salted bomb, carrying two vials of radioactive cobalt-57. It contaminated a large area in the Chihuahuan Desert near Mapimí in Mexico's Durango state, requiring years of cleanup.

14 At Riverfront Stadium, the National League wins its eighth straight Major League Baseball All-Star Game, a 12-inning 5–4 victory. Pete Rose crashes into Cleveland Indians catcher Ray Fosse to score the winning run on Jim Hickman's single. Claude Osteen pitches the 10th for the win, and Carl Yastrzemski of the Boston Red Sox captures the MVP trophy for the American League.

16 | Three Rivers Stadium in Pittsburgh opened as 46,846 paying customers watched the Pittsburgh Pirates lose to the Cincinnati Reds, 3 to 2.

20 | "Lucy the Elephant", a 60 feet (18 m) tall wooden landmark in Margate City, New Jersey made in the shape of an elephant, was moved to a new location after having originally been slated for demolition in order to clear the way for the building of a condominium. The building, one of the most unusual in the United States, had been a fixture since its construction by James V. Lafferty in 1881 and was saved after a committee of Margate citizens raised funds to have it transported two blocks to city-owned property.

25 | The U.S. Navy postponed its first ever submarine launch of the multiple-warhead Poseidon missile, the day after a Soviet Russian fishing trawler came within 200 yards (180 m) of the American sub USS James Madison during a trial run. The encounter came in international waters 30 miles (48 km) east of Florida; the "fishing boat" was believed by the U.S. to have electronic equipment used to gather data on the submarine and the new missile.

July

26 | Wally Scott and another pilot, Ben Greene, broke the world record for distance flown in an unpowered aircraft, flying separate sailplanes a distance of 716.95 miles (1,153.82 km). Scott and Greene were released over Odessa, Texas, and touched down nine hours later in Columbus, Nebraska, breaking the 1964 record of 647.17 miles (1,041.52 km) set by Al Parker.

27 | In Chicago, Sears, Roebuck & Company announced its plan to construct the tallest building in the world, to be 1,450 feet (440 m) high, taller than the 1,350 feet (410 m) twin towers of the World Trade Center in New York City The 110-story Sears Tower (now called the Willis Tower) would take its first tenants in 1973 and would remain the world's tallest building for until 1998, when the 1,483 feet (452 m) tall Petronas Towers would open in Malaysia.

30 | For the first time, players in the National Football League voted to walk out on strike after a vote by the 1,200 veteran's players in the National Football League Players Association (NFLPA). While rookies showed up at NFL training camps, most veterans elected to stay away.

August

2 | For the first time, a "jumbo jet" was hijacked. Pan American Flight 299, which had made the first commercial Boeing 747 flight, was on its way from New York to San Juan, Puerto Rico. Shortly after midnight, one of the 360 passengers commandeered the aircraft brandished a gun and threatened to detonate explosives in his carry-on luggage and demanded to be flown to Havana. Cuba's Premier Fidel Castro traveled to the Jose Marti Airport to discuss plans for the 747 pilot about how to safely take off from the airport's runways, which were not long enough to accommodate a large jet. The 747 took off for Miami after one hour in Cuba and safely returned. The aircraft, N736PA and designated as "Clipper Victor", would be destroyed in 1977 in the Tenerife airport disaster, after being struck by another Boeing 747 in the deadliest aviation disaster in history.

3 | The United States Navy submarine USS James Madison made the first successful underwater test of the multi-warhead Poseidon C3 nuclear missile. Madison launched the unarmed missile skyward from a depth of 120 feet (37 m) and the rocket traveled 2,880 miles (4,630 km) to its intended target in the South Atlantic Ocean. Another U.S. Navy ship, the destroyer escort USS Calcaterra, positioned itself between the launch site and a Soviet surveillance trawler, the Leptev, to prevent close observation or the retrieval of debris from the launch. The Poseidon C3 missile was cleared by the Navy on March 31, 1971, for deployment aboard all ten of the James Madison-class submarines and the nine of the Lafayette-class submarines.

6   A bill to create the independent United States Postal Service (USPS), and to abolish the existing United States Post Office Department, passed Congress after being approved by the U.S. House of Representatives, 339 to 29. The bill, proposed by U.S. President Nixon, had passed the U.S. Senate earlier and marked "the most sweeping reform in the postal system's 181 year history" in the United States. The U.S. Senate had voted, 57 to 7, to approve the bill on August 3 President Nixon signed the bill on August 12, authorizing the transfer of functions to the USPS effective July 1, 1971.

10   The 232 prisoners housed on the ninth floor of the overcrowded Manhattan House of Detention, colloquially known as "The Tombs, took five guards hostage at daybreak and demanded reforms a meeting with Mayor John V. Lindsay. At the time, the facility had a maximum capacity of 932 men for its small cells, and had almost 3,000 detained in filthy conditions, many of whom had been awaiting a court date for months. The prisoners released their hostages, unharmed, after a pledge from the city that they would not be prosecuted for the takeover, and the overcrowding would be eased by the transfer of inmates to other prisons in the state.

13   Massachusetts became the first state in the United States to enact no-fault insurance in motor-vehicle accidents. Ignoring threats of ceasing business in the state by its four insurance companies, Governor Francis W. Sargent signed the bill at 8:10 in the evening during a televised news conference in Boston, providing for the law to become effective on January 1, 1971 Under the scheme, now universal in the U.S., a person's own insurance would pay for the initial medical expenses and damages for lost work for an injured person up to a limit (initially $2,000 USD) and the carrier would then seek recovery from the insurance carrier of the driver at fault, if there was another vehicle involved. Puerto Rico had enacted a no-fault plan in 1969.

14   All diet foods and drinks with sodium cyclamate as an artificial sweetener were banned in the United States. The United States Food and Drug Administration gave retailers 18 days to sell or remove their remaining stock of the cyclamate-sweetened diet products by September 1. The compounds commercially referred to as "cyclamates" or "Scary", had been found, in 1969, to cause cancer in laboratory tests on animals. Extrapolating the data to human beings, a scientific study had concluded that consuming more than 168 mg of cyclamates per day was hazardous. Bottles and cans of Cyclamate-sweeten diet soft drinks had been banned since January 1, but the sweeteners were still used in powdered mixes for lemonade, fruit drinks and iced tea.

18   The United States disposed of 418 containers of nerve gas by loading it onto the retired U.S. Navy ship SS LeBaron Russell Briggs, then sinking the ship in Atlantic Ocean waters 3 miles (4.8 km) deep at an American munitions dump 283 miles (455 km) east of Florida. The total cargo of the 418 drums was 12,540 rockets of Sarin (GB nerve gas) and a single canister of the more potent VX nerve gas.

23   Lightning strikes in the U.S. state of Washington ignited 225 individual fires that soon merged into a major forest fire that burned 190 square miles (490 km2) of the Wenatchee National Forest over a period of two weeks. Heavy rains extinguished the blaze in the Entiat Mountains, dubbed the "Entiat Fire", on September 7, after the involvement of 8,500 firefighters to prevent the conflagration from spreading further.

29   The McDonnell Douglas DC-10, a "jumbo jet" to rival the Boeing 747, made its first flight. A crew of four, led by pilot Clifford Stout, was on board when the tri-jet DC-10 took off from the airport at Long Beach, California at 10:00 in the morning and flew for several hours before landing at 1:26 at Edwards Air Force Base. Designed to be produce less noise than most aircraft, and with room to seat 345 passengers, the aircraft would go into service on August 5, 1971.

September

5 Operation Jefferson Glenn ran from 5 September 1970 to 8 October 1971 and was the last major operation in which U.S. ground forces participated during the Vietnam War and the final major offensive in which the 101st Airborne Division fought. This was a joint military operation combining forces of the 101st Airborne and the Army of the Republic of Vietnam (ARVN) 1st Infantry Division.

6 The Popular Front for the Liberation of Palestine hijacks 4 passenger aircraft from Pan Am, TWA and Swissair on flights to New York from Brussels, Frankfurt and Zürich.

7 An anti-war rally is held at Valley Forge, Pennsylvania, attended by Jane Fonda, Donald Sutherland and future Democratic presidential nominee John Kerry.

9 Elvis Presley begins his first concert tour since 1958, in Phoenix, Arizona at the Veterans Memorial Coliseum.

10 The Chevrolet Vega is introduced. The Chevrolet Vega is a subcompact automobile that was manufactured and marketed by GM's Chevrolet subdivision from 1970 to 1977. Available in two-door hatchback, notchback, wagon, and sedan delivery body styles, all models were powered by an inline four-cylinder engine with a lightweight, aluminum alloy cylinder block. The Vega first went on sale in Chevrolet dealerships on September 10, 1970.

11 The Ford Pinto is introduced.

September

13 The first New York City Marathon was held 49 years ago on September 13, 1970, organized by New York Road Runners presidents; Fred Lebow and Vincent Chiappetta, with 127 competitors running several loops around the Park Drive of Central Park. Only about 100 spectators watched Gary Muhrcke win the race in 2:31:38. In fact, a total of only 55 runners crossed the finish line. Over the years, the marathon grew larger and larger. To celebrate the U.S. bicentennial in 1976, city auditor George Spitz proposed that the race traverse all five boroughs. With the support of Manhattan Borough President Percy Sutton, the men convinced Mayor Beame and, eventually, race director Fred Lebow. The race was a huge success, and what was intended as a one-time celebration, became the annual course.

18 Jimi Hendrix dies aged just 27 years old in London, due to alcohol-related complications. Born in Seattle, Washington, Hendrix began playing guitar at age 15. In 1961, he enlisted in the US Army and trained as a paratrooper in the 101st Airborne Division, but he was discharged the following year. He moved to Clarksville, Tennessee soon after and began playing gigs on the Chitlin' Circuit, earning a place in the Isley Brothers' backing band and later with Little Richard, with whom he continued to work through mid-1965. He played with Curtis Knight and the Squires before moving to England in late 1966 after being discovered by Linda Keith, who interested bassist Chas Chandler of the Animals in becoming his first manager. Within months, Hendrix earned three UK top ten hits with the Jimi Hendrix Experience: "Hey Joe", "Purple Haze", and "The Wind Cries Mary". He achieved fame in the US after his performance at the Monterey Pop Festival in 1967, and his third and final studio album Electric Ladyland reached number one in the US in 1968; it was Hendrix's most commercially successful release and his only number-one album. He was the world's highest-paid performer, and he headlined the Woodstock Festival in 1969 and the Isle of Wight Festival in 1970. He died from barbiturate-related asphyxia on September 18, 1970, at age 27.

26 The Laguna Fire, previously known as the Kitchen Creek Fire and the Boulder Oaks Fire, occurred in 1970 in the Laguna Mountains and East County region of San Diego County in Southern California, United States. It was the third-largest wildfire in the history of California at that time, after the Santiago Canyon Fire of 1889, and the Matilija Fire of 1932. It was one of many wildfires in a massive conflagration that spanned across the state from September 22 to October 4, 1970. The Laguna Fire of 1970 caused at least $234 million (1970 USD) in damages, including $5.6 million of damage to residential property.

September

27 | Richard Nixon begins a tour of Europe, visiting Italy, Yugoslavia, Spain, the United Kingdom and Ireland.

29 | The U.S. Congress gives President Richard Nixon authority to sell arms to Israel.

October

2 | The Wichita State University football team's "Gold" plane crashes in Colorado, killing most of the players. They were on their way (along with administrators and fans) to a game with Utah State University.

4 | On Sunday afternoon, October 4, 1970, producer Paul Rothchild became concerned when Joplin failed to show up at Sunset Sound Recorders for a recording session in which she was scheduled to provide the vocal track for the instrumental track of the song "Buried Alive in the Blues". In the evening, Full Tilt Boogie's road manager, John Cooke, drove to the Landmark Motor Hotel in Hollywood where Joplin was staying. He saw Joplin's psychedelically painted Porsche 356 C Cabriolet in the parking lot and upon entering Joplin's room (#105), he found her dead on the floor beside her bed. The official cause of death was a heroin overdose, possibly compounded by alcohol. Cooke believes Joplin had been given heroin that was much more potent than normal, as several of her dealer's other customers also overdosed that week. Her death was ruled as accidental.

8 | Vietnam War: In Paris, a Communist delegation rejects U.S. President Richard Nixon's October 7 peace proposal as "a maneuver to deceive world opinion."

12 | Vietnam War: U.S. President Richard Nixon announces that the United States will withdraw 40,000 more troops before Christmas.

21 | A U.S. Air Force plane makes an emergency landing near Leninakan, Soviet Union. The Soviets release the American officers, including two generals, November 10.

23 | Gary Gabelich broke the LSR by achieving average speeds of 622.407 mph (1,001.667 km/h) over a flying mile and 630.388 mph (1,014.511 km/h) over a flying kilometer. The thrust used during this attempt was between 13,000 pounds (5,900 kilograms) and 15,000 pounds (6,800 kilograms). A top speed of approximately 650 mph (1,050 km/h) was momentarily attained during one run.

The FIA rules dictate that a land speed mark is recognized only after two runs through the FIA measured kilometer and mile courses. The two corresponding speeds are then averaged for the official time and speed. Additionally both runs must be made within one hour.

Gabelich averaged 629.412 mph (1,013 km/h) on his first run and 631.367 mph (1,016 km/h) on his second run for an average speed of 630.388 mph (1,015 km/h) establishing a new kilometer FIA LSR. The mile FIA LSR was the first exceeding 1,000 km/h (621 mph) and remained unbeaten until 1983, when Richard Noble broke it driving Thrust 2. The faster kilometer FIA LSR remained unbroken for 27 years when ThrustSSC went supersonic in 1997.

25 | The wreck of the Confederate submarine Hunley is found off Charleston, South Carolina, by pioneer underwater archaeologist, Dr. E. Lee Spence, and then just 22 years old. Hunley was the first submarine in history to sink a ship in warfare.

November

3 Democrats sweep the U.S. Congressional midterm elections; Ronald Reagan is re-elected governor of California; Jimmy Carter is elected governor of Georgia.

5 Vietnam War: The United States Military Assistance Command in Vietnam reports the lowest weekly American soldier death toll in five years (24 soldiers die that week, which is the fifth consecutive week the death toll is below 50; 431 are reported wounded that week, however).

8 Tom Dempsey, who was born with a deformed right foot and right hand, sets a National Football League record by kicking a 63-yard field goal to lift the New Orleans Saints to a 19–17 victory over the Detroit Lions at Tulane Stadium.

9 The Supreme Court of the United States votes 6–3 not to hear a case by the state of Massachusetts, about the constitutionality of a state law granting Massachusetts residents the right to refuse military service in an undeclared war.

10 Vietnam War – Vietnamization: For the first time in five years, an entire week ends with no reports of United States combat fatalities in Southeast Asia.

14 Southern Airways Flight 932 crashes in Wayne County, West Virginia; all 75 on board, including 37 players and 5 coaches from the Marshall University football team, are killed.

16 The Lockheed L-1011 TriStar flies for the first time.

17 Lieutenant William Calley goes on trial for the My Lai Massacre.

18 U.S. President Richard Nixon asks the U.S. Congress for US$155 million in supplemental aid for the Cambodian government (US$85 million is for military assistance to prevent the overthrow of the government of Premier Lon Nol by the Khmer Rouge and North Vietnam).

November

21 Vietnam War – Operation Ivory Coast: A joint Air Force and Army team raids the Sơn Tây prison camp in an attempt to free American POWs thought to be held there (no Americans are killed, but the prisoners have already moved to another camp; all U.S. POWs are moved to a handful of central prison complexes as a result of this raid).

23 Rodgers and Hammerstein's Oklahoma! makes its network TV debut, when CBS telecasts the 1955 film version as a three-hour Thanksgiving special.

December

2 The Environmental Protection Agency (EPA) is an independent agency of the United States federal government for environmental protection. President Richard Nixon proposed the establishment of EPA on July 9, 1970 and it began operation on December 2, 1970, after Nixon signed an executive order. The order establishing the EPA was ratified by committee hearings in the House and Senate.

19 The final episode of H.R. Pufnstuf, An Old Fashioned Christmas, airs on NBC.

23 The North Tower of the World Trade Center is topped out at 1,368 feet (417 m), making it the tallest building in the world.

29 The Occupational Safety and Health Act of 1970 is a US labor law governing the federal law of occupational health and safety in the private sector and federal government in the United States. It was enacted by Congress in 1970 and was signed by President Richard Nixon on December 29, 1970. Its main goal is to ensure that employers provide employees with an environment free from recognized hazards, such as exposure to toxic chemicals, excessive noise levels, mechanical dangers, heat or cold stress, or unsanitary conditions.

The New Honda 70.

This is the bike for practical men and women who want to beat the traffic. Easy to ride—three-speed transmission with a fully-automatic clutch. Easy upkeep—you can get close to 200 mpg. And a little Honda 72cc four-stroke OHC single-cylinder engine that packs a lot more power than you might expect— 5.0 bhp @ 8,500 rpm. That's enough power for a top speed of 50 mph. You can start the CM-70 with its kick starter or simply by pushing a button. And there are tough, sure Honda brakes, front and rear, to let you stop safely. With its large headlight, turn signals and taillights, the Honda 70's ready to travel. And with its snappy colors — red, blue or green — it's ready to travel in style. So what are you waiting for? Get a new Honda CM-70. And get around town with it soon.

© 1970 American Honda Motor Co., Inc.

From Mighty to Mini, Honda has it all.

Always ride safely. Wear a helmet and observe all rules of the road.

"Ever notice how colds feel worse at night?"

"Maybe it's my imagination. "But in the wee small hours, a sneeze or cough can sound like a thunderclap. And the later it gets, the more my aches and pains ache and pain.

"To avoid all that, I use NyQuil.

"NyQuil helps relieve sniffles, sneezes, and stuffed-up noses; eases aches and pains; soothes minor throat irritations; in fact, relieves all these major cold symptoms for hours.

"As a result, when you get NyQuil, you also get the one other thing your cold really needs: a good night's rest.

"Believe me, it's nice for a change to go to bed with a cold and wake up feeling better."

Vicks NyQuil. The night-time colds medicine.

24

McDonald's Corporation is an American fast food company, founded in 1940 as a restaurant operated by Richard and Maurice McDonald, in San Bernardino, California, United States. They rechristened their business as a hamburger stand, and later turned the company into a franchise, with the Golden Arches logo being introduced in 1953 at a location in Phoenix, Arizona. In 1955, Ray Kroc, a businessman, joined the company as a franchise agent and proceeded to purchase the chain from the McDonald brothers. McDonald's had its original headquarters in Oak Brook, Illinois, but moved its global headquarters to Chicago in early 2018.

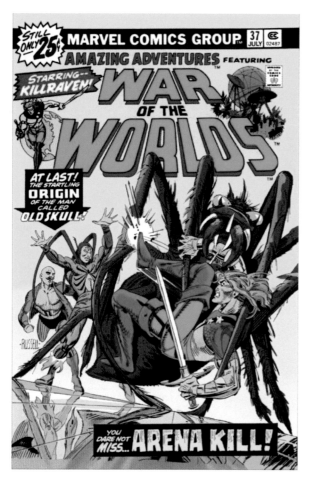

You'll be *happier* with a HOOVER

Whichever type you prefer

Model 28 . . . *Hoover's new popular-priced Triple-Action Cleaner, with the exclusive Hoover cleaning principle—it beats, as it sweeps, as it cleans. Rolls easily. Gets deep-down dirt to prolong rug life. Keeps rug colors bright* **$74.95**
Cleaning tools in handy kit $19.95

Think of how seldom you buy a cleaner, and think of how often you use it. So think before you buy. Everyone knows that Hoover is the best. Forty years of manufacture and more than eight million Hoovers sold have proved it. Why take less than Hoover when it offers you a complete choice—two types, four models. Call your Hoover dealer now for a home showing of any model.

Get happier today

Model 50 . . . *Hoover's great new cylinder cleaner. Easiest-to-use cleaner of its type. Cleans by powerful suction. Features include the exclusive new Dirt Ejector, end and top carrying handles. Complete with cleaning tools in handy kit, including Mothimizer and sprayer* **$79.50**

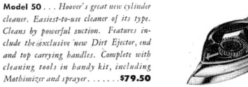

Get happier ironing, too. See the great new Hoover Iron at leading stores. "Feel" the difference. So light, slick, quick, well balanced. Exclusive easy-to-read Pancake Dial gives positive heat control. Fast, even heat in every inch of ironing surface.

Model 115, *Hoover, Junior. Low and trim, it is ideal for small homes, handy for all homes. Cleans far bigger than its size. With Hoover's exclusive Triple Action —it beats, as it sweeps, as it cleans. Only* **$59.95**
Cleaning tools extra.

THE HOOVER COMPANY, *North Canton, Ohio; Hamilton, Ontario, Canada; Perivale, England*

How Sir Ranulph Fiennes is always in the right place at the right time.

Whether in Saharan sands or in frozen arctic wastes, Sir Ranulph Fiennes would never set out without his Rolex. "I've navigated across the world, right through both Poles with it," he explains.

For Sir Ranulph knows precisely what angle his shadow will fall at in any given hour, so he can deduce the direction in which to proceed, despite the absence of landmarks.

He wears a GMT-Master which, "has never let me down, in all those years."

When asked whether he would ever consider embarking on an expedition with a different watch, Sir Ranulph's reply, although terse, is in fact a supreme compliment. "Oh no," he says briskly. "I think that would be a very stupid risk to take."

The Rolex GMT-Master.

ROLEX
of Geneva

1970 Rolex GMT Master ref. 1675, 40mm. Unpolished 40mm. case and Pepsi bezel. The Rolex GMT-Master was developed in cooperation with Pan Am as an aviator watch. The introduced fourth hand allowed the display of an additional time with the corresponding number markings on the outer bezel. Pilots used the second time to display the Greenwich Mean Time (GMT), which led to the name Rolex GMT Master.

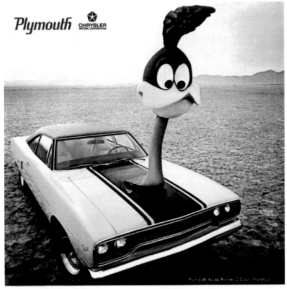

Tonight...a sparkling Babycham

COST OF LIVING IN 1970

Looking back at 1970, it often seems that times were simpler then. No one was tethered to a cell phone or computer and kids still went outside to play after school. Prices, of course, were a lot lower in 1970 as well, thanks to a lower cost of living. Of course, everything is relative, as they say. Individuals made a lot less at their jobs so, therefore, things cost less.

Nevertheless, it's fun to look back at days gone by and marvel at the cost of things like homes, cars, and common household items as well as college tuitions and other major expenses.

Peruse the figures below for a sampling of typical 1970 prices.

Food / Toiletries

Large eggs – 59 cents per dozen

Milk – 62 cents per gallon

Potatoes – 99 cents for 10 lbs.

Apples - 4Lbs 59 Cents

Dog Food - 12 Cans $1.00

Butter - $1.33 per pound

Bacon – 80 cents per pound

Sirloin Steak - $1.19 per pound

Loaf of bread – 25 cents

Ketchup – 19 cents

Sugar – 39 cents for 5 lbs.

Tomato Soup – 10 cents per can

Coffee - $1.90 per pound

Toothpaste – 75 cents

Head and Shoulder Shampoo 79 Cents

Pork Chops – 59 cents per pound

Pot Roast – 59 cents per pound

Frozen TV dinners – 39 cents

Bar Soap – 20 cents per bar

Onions – 9 cents per pound

1970 Clothing Prices

Men's down jacket - $20

Men's suit - $40

Men's sport coat - $30

Men's dress shoes - $22

Wrangler jeans - $10

Women's summer dress - $8

Striped Ladies Flare Pants and Tunic $10.00

Women's slippers - $4

Ladies spring coat - $25

1970 Furniture / Household prices

Bunk beds - $100

Recliner chair - $70

Bean Bag chair - $20

Porcelain sink - $10

Mattress and box spring - $75

Latex house paint - $7 per gallon

Toys prices in the 1970s

Atari game cartridges - $20

Mattel Hot Wheels Car – 69 cents

Radio-Controlled car - $5

United States postage Stamp 6 cents

Average Income per year $9,400.00

Barbie inflatable furniture set - $2

1 Carat Diamond Ring $299

Chair La-Z-Boy Rocker Recliner $188.00

Back To College Typewriter $28.88

Barbie Doll $4.77

25" Cinema Screen Color TV $739.95

Lava lamp $19.95

Set Of Tube Furniture $59.99

Schaefer Pen $9.95

Man's Westclox Watch $18.00

Average Cost of new house $23,450.00

Average Monthly Rent $140.00

Car-related Items

Chrysler Newport $3861

AMC Gremlin $1879

Gas – 36 cents per gallon

CB Radio - $140

Whitewall Tires - $13

Motor Oil – 25 cents per quart

8-track tape player - $40

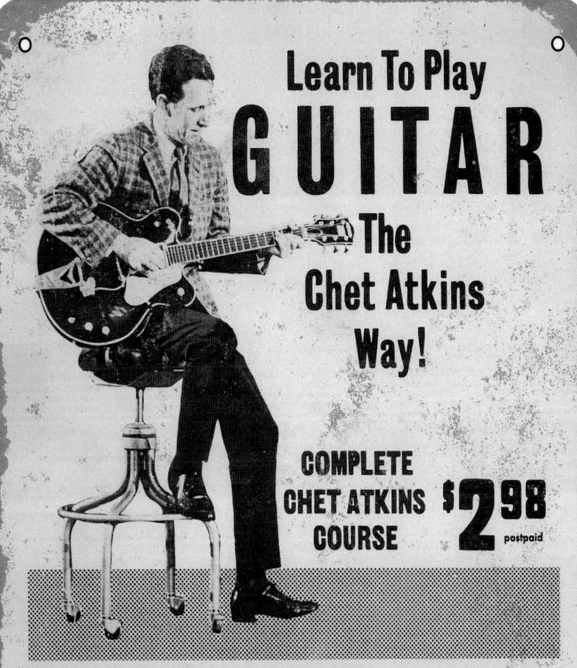

Learn To Play GUITAR
The Chet Atkins Way!

COMPLETE CHET ATKINS COURSE $2.98 postpaid

BIRTHS OF 1970

Matthew Brandon Ross born January 3, 1970 is an American actor, director, and screenwriter. He wrote and directed the feature film Captain Fantastic, starring Viggo Mortensen, for which he won Un Certain Regard at the 2016 Cannes Film Festival. Before that, Ross made seven short films, including The Language of Love, which premiered at the Sundance Film Festival.

As an actor, Ross's roles have included Gavin Belson in the HBO series Silicon Valley, Alby Grant in the HBO series Big Love, Glenn Odekirk in The Aviator, and Luis Carruthers in American Psycho. He was also Eddie Scott in the 2005 film Good Night, and Good Luck, for which he was nominated for a Screen Actors Guild Award for Outstanding Performance by a Cast in a Motion Picture. He also directed the feature film 28 Hotel Rooms, which premiered at the Sundance Film Festival. In 2011 and 2015, he played Charles Montgomery in the first and fifth seasons of FX's anthology series American Horror Story.

Christopher Morgan Klucsarits was born January 4, 1970 and passed away April 2, 2010. He was an American professional wrestler. He was best known for his appearances with the professional wrestling promotions World Championship Wrestling (WCW) and the World Wrestling Federation (WWF) from 1995 to 2004 under the ring names Chris Kanyon, Kanyon, and Mortis. Kanyon debuted in World Championship Wrestling (WCW) as a jobber. After several months he was placed with Mark Starr in a tag team called "Men at Work". Their gimmick was that they were two construction workers turned wrestlers who wore jeans to the ring, and that Kanyon would cause the team to suffer losses by taking measurements with his tape measure at inopportune times. Kanyon was replaced with Mike Winner before the team disbanded altogether. Kanyon had been suffering from bipolar disorder, and he threatened suicide in the weeks prior to his death. On April 2, 2010, his brother Ken Klucsarits found him dead in his Sunnyside, Queens, New York apartment with an empty bottle of antidepressants.

Julie Suzanne Chen Moonves born January 6, 1970 is an American television personality, news anchor, and producer for CBS. She has been the host of the U.S. version of the CBS reality-television program Big Brother since its debut in July 2000 and is the longest-serving host of any country's version of the show. Chen Moonves was a co-host and the moderator of the CBS Daytime talk show, The Talk, for eight seasons. Previously, she was a co-anchor of The Early Show on CBS. One of her earlier jobs came in June 1990, interning at CBS Morning News alongside Andy Cohen – the series which she would anchor a decade later. In 2015, Chen revealed on The Talk that during her time in Dayton her news director had told her that she would never become a news anchor because of her "Asian eyes". After a "big-time agent" agreed and advised her to get plastic surgery, she made the decision to have a surgical procedure to reduce the epicanthic folds of her eyes.

Zacharias Manuel de la Rocha was born in Long Beach, California, on January 12, 1970. De la Rocha met Tim Commerford in elementary school, and in junior high school, they both played guitar in a band called Juvenile Expression. De la Rocha's interest in punk rock bands like The Clash, The Misfits, Sex Pistols, and Bad Religion turned into an appreciation for other bands like Minor Threat, Bad Brains, and The Teen Idols. In high school, he joined the straight edge band Hard Stance, which evolved into the hardcore band Inside Out around 1988 and gained a national underground following.

Tom Morello recruited former Greta drummer Brad Wilk—who had previously auditioned for Lock Up before that band's dissolution earlier that same year—and de la Rocha recruited his former Juvenile Expression bandmate, Tim Commerford, to play bass. The band was named for an unreleased Inside Out record, Rage Against the Machine.

Matthew Lyn Lillard born January 24, 1970 is an American actor, voice actor, director, and producer. Matthew Lillard was born in Lansing, Michigan. After high school, Lillard was co-host of a short-lived TV show titled SK8-TV, and afterwards was hired as an extra in Ghoulies 3: Ghoulies Go to College (1991). In 1994, he was cast in the John Waters black comedy Serial Mom.

Lillard was cast as Shaggy Rogers in the 2002 live-action Scooby-Doo film, a role he later reprised in the 2004 sequel Scooby-Doo 2: Monsters Unleashed. When Casey Kasem, who had voiced the character from the show's debut in 1969, retired due to declining health in 2009, Lillard was chosen as his replacement and voiced Shaggy in the two subsequent animated series, Mystery Incorporated and Be Cool Scooby-Doo!, as well as every direct-to-video film since 2010's Scooby-Doo! Abracadabra-Doo. In 2012, Lillard guest starred in the Criminal Minds episode "The Apprenticeship". The following year, he played the role of Daniel Frye on the American TV series The Bridge.

Heather Joan Graham born January 29, 1970 is an American actress, director, and writer. Graham's first film appearance was an uncredited cameo in Mrs. Soffel (1984). Her first credited film appearance was in the television film Student Exchange. In 1986, she appeared on a special "Teen Week" episode of the NBC game show Scrabble. Then she appeared in numerous television commercials and an episode of the sitcom Growing Pains in 1987. After appearing in television commercials, her first starring role in a feature film came with the teen comedy License to Drive (1988), followed by the critically acclaimed film Drugstore Cowboy (1989), which gained her initial industry notice. She then played supporting roles in films such as Shout (1991), Diggstown (1992), Six Degrees of Separation (1993), Swingers (1996) and on the television series Twin Peaks (1991) and its prequel film Fire Walk with Me (1992), before gaining critical praise for starring in Paul Thomas Anderson's Boogie Nights (1997) as porn starlet Brandy / Rollergirl. In 1999, she co-starred in Bowfinger and Austin Powers: The Spy Who Shagged Me.

Alonzo Harding Mourning Jr. born February 8, 1970 is an American former professional basketball player. Mourning played most of his 15-year National Basketball Association career for the Miami Heat.
Nicknamed "Zo", Mourning played at center. Following his college basketball career at Georgetown University, his tenacity on defense twice earned him NBA Defensive Player of the Year Award and perennially placed him on the NBA All-Defensive Team.
Mourning made a comeback after undergoing a kidney transplant and later won the 2006 NBA Championship with the Heat. Mourning also played for the Charlotte Hornets and New Jersey Nets. On March 30, 2009, Mourning became the first Miami Heat player to have his number retired. Since June 26, 2009, Mourning has served as Vice President of Player Programs and Development for the Heat. In 2010, Mourning was inducted into the Virginia Sports Hall of Fame.

Bellamy Young born Amy Maria Young on February 19, 1970. She is an American actress and singer, best known for her role as Melody "Mellie" Grant in the ABC drama series Scandal. In 1995, Young made her television debut in a recurring role on the NBC daytime soap opera Another World as Dr. Courtney Evans. She guest-starred on Law & Order in 1997 and 1998, in two different roles. In 2000's she began appearing in guest-starring roles on a number of television dramas and comedies, including The Drew Carey Show, The X Files, ER, Frasier, The West Wing, NCIS, Medium, Grey's Anatomy, Private Practice, Two and a Half Men, Supernatural, Drop Dead Diva, and Castle. From 2000 to 2011, Young made over 30 guest appearances on television shows. In 2016, she starred in the crime drama film The Night Stalker directed by Megan Griffiths about the serial killer Richard Ramirez. The following year, she had a supporting role in the independent comedy film Bernard and Huey opposite Jim Rash and David Koechner.

Nicole Julianne Sullivan born April 21, 1970 is an American actress, voice artist and comedian. She has played a recurring character, Jill Tracy, on Scrubs and voiced the heroic Mira Nova in Disney/Pixar's Buzz Lightyear of Star Command and the villainous Shego in Disney's Kim Possible. She had recurring voice roles on Family Guy and voiced "Franny Robinson" in Disney's Meet the Robinsons. From 2008 to 2009, Sullivan starred in and was the lead of her own Lifetime television series Rita Rocks.

From 2008 to 2013, she voiced Marlene in The Penguins of Madagascar. Sullivan played Jules' (Courteney Cox) therapist, Lynn Mettler, on the comedy Cougar Town. She portrayed Lyla in the Disney Channel original movie Let It Shine in 2012. In 2013, she starred in the short-lived Nickelodeon sitcom Wendell and Vinnie as Wilma Basset. Since 2014, she has portrayed Janine, the Johnsons' next-door neighbor, on the ABC sitcom Black-ish. Also Disjointed starring Kathy Bates.

Jason Michael Lee born April 25, 1970. He is an American actor, comedian, producer, writer, skateboarder and photographer. He is best known for his role as Earl Hickey in the television comedy series My Name Is Earl, for which he was nominated for Best Actor in a Musical or Comedy TV series in 2005 and 2006 by The Golden Globes. Before he became an actor, Lee was known as a professional skateboarder in the late 1980s and early 1990s. In 1992, he founded Stereo Sound Agency, known as Stereo Skateboards, with fellow skater Chris "Dune" Pastras. In 2003, after it had been defunct for a few years, the pair successfully revived the company. In 2005, Lee was offered the lead role in My Name Is Earl. According to interviews on the first-season DVD, he passed on the series twice before finally agreeing to read for the pilot. In the series, he stars as Earl Hickey. Lee received two Golden Globe nominations for Best Performance by an Actor in a Television Series – Musical or Comedy in 2006 and 2007, as well as a nomination for the Screen Actors Guild Award for Outstanding Performance by a Male.

Sean Patrick Hayes born June 26, 1970 is an American actor, comedian, singer and producer. He is best known for his role as Jack McFarland on the NBC sitcom Will & Grace, for which he won a Primetime Emmy Award, four SAG Awards, and one American Comedy Award, and earned six Golden Globe nominations. He also runs a television production company called Hazy Mills Productions, which produces shows such as Grimm, Hot in Cleveland, The Soul Man, and Hollywood Game Night. He is known for his film work in movies such as Billy's Hollywood Screen Kiss, Cats & Dogs, Pieces of April, The Cat in the Hat, Win a Date with Tad Hamilton!, The Bucket List, and The Three Stooges.

He is also known for his work on Broadway such as An Act of God and Promises, Promises, where he played Chuck Baxter and received a nomination for Tony Award for Best Performance by a Leading Actor in a Musical. He has hosted the 64th Tony Awards, for which he was awarded a Primetime Emmy Award for Outstanding Special Class Program.

River Jude Phoenix was born August 23, 1970 and passed away October 31, 1993. He was an American actor, musician, and animal activist. Phoenix's work encompassed 24 films and television appearances, and his rise to fame led to his status as a "teen idol". He began his acting career at age 10, in television commercials. He starred in the science fiction adventure film Explorers (1985) and had his first notable role in 1986's Stand by Me, a coming-of-age film based on the novella The Body by Stephen King. Phoenix made a transition into more adult-oriented roles with Running on Empty (1988), playing the son of fugitive parents in a well-received performance that earned him a nomination for an Academy Award for Best Supporting Actor, and My Own Private Idaho (1991), playing a gay hustler in search of his estranged mother. On October 31, 1993, Phoenix collapsed and died of combined drug intoxication following a drug overdose on the sidewalk outside the West Hollywood nightclub The Viper Room at the age of 23. At the time of his death, Phoenix was acting in Dark Blood, which was released in 2012.

Jo Dee Marie Messina born August 25, 1970. She is an American country music artist. She has charted six number one singles on the Billboard country music charts. She has been honored by the Country Music Association, the Academy of Country Music and has been nominated for two Grammy Awards. She was the first female country artist to score three multiple-week Number One songs from the same album. To date, she has two Platinum and three Gold-certified albums by the RIAA.

Messina debuted in 1996 with the single Heads Carolina, Tails California. Her album was certified Gold by the RIAA. Her second album, I'm Alright, produced five Top 10 Country hits between 1998 and 1999, and sold over a million copies in America. Since her debut, six of her singles have peaked at No. 1 on the Billboard Country singles chart and five of her albums have received a certification by the RIAA or the CRIA. She has sold over 5 million records worldwide.

Matthew Paige Damon born October 8, 1970. He is an American actor, film producer and screenwriter. Born and raised in Cambridge, Massachusetts, Damon began his acting career by appearing in high school theater productions. He made his professional acting debut in the film Mystic Pizza (1988).

He came to prominence in 1997, when he wrote and starred in Good Will Hunting, alongside Ben Affleck, which won them the Academy and Golden Globe awards for Best Screenplay and earned Damon a nomination for the Academy Award for Best Actor. He continued to garner praise from critics for his roles as the eponymous character in Saving Private Ryan (1998), the antihero in The Talented Mr. Ripley (1999), a fallen angel in Dogma (1999) and Jay and Silent Bob Reboot (2019), an energy analyst in Syriana (2005), and a corrupt Irish-American police officer in The Departed (2006). Damon is also known for his starring roles as Jason Bourne in the Bourne franchise (2002–2016) and as a con man in the Ocean's trilogy (2001–2007).

Jennifer Lynn Connelly born December 12, 1970. She is an American actress who began her career as a child model. She made her film acting debut in the crime film Once Upon a Time in America. Connelly continued modeling and acting, starring in a number of films, including the horror film Phenomena, the musical fantasy film Labyrinth, the romantic comedy Career Opportunities, and the period superhero film The Rocketeer. She gained critical acclaim for her work in the science fiction film Dark City and for playing a drug addict in Darren Aronofsky's drama Requiem for a Dream. In 2002, Connelly won the Academy Award for Best Supporting Actress for portraying Alicia Nash in Ron Howard's biopic A Beautiful Mind. Jennifer was named Amnesty International Ambassador for Human Rights Education in 2005. She has been the face of Balenciaga fashion advertisements, as well as for Revlon cosmetics. In 2012, she was named the first global face of the Shiseido Company. Magazines, including Time, Vanity Fair and Esquire, as well as the Los Angeles Times newspaper, have included her on their lists of the world's most beautiful women.

SPORTING EVENTS

Super Bowl IV

Minnesota Vikings

7

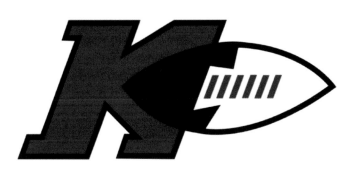

Kansas City Chiefs

23

Super Bowl IV, the fourth and final AFL-NFL World Championship Game in professional American football, was played on January 11, 1970, at Tulane Stadium in New Orleans, Louisiana. The American Football League (AFL) champion Kansas City Chiefs defeated the National Football League (NFL) champion Minnesota Vikings by the score of 23–7. This victory by the AFL squared the Super Bowl series with the NFL at two games apiece as the two leagues merged into one after the game.

Despite the AFL's New York Jets winning the previous season's Super Bowl, many sports writers and fans thought it was a fluke and continued to believe that the NFL was still superior to the AFL, and thus fully expected the Vikings to defeat the Chiefs; the Vikings entered the Super Bowl as 12½ to 13½-point favorites. Minnesota posted a 12–2 record in 1969, then defeated the Los Angeles Rams 23–20 for the Western Conference title, and the Cleveland Browns 27–7 in the NFL Championship Game. The Chiefs, who previously appeared in the first Super Bowl, finished the regular season at 11–3; they continued with two road wins in the AFL playoffs, dethroning the New York Jets 13–6, and then taking down division rival Oakland Raiders 17–7 in the final AFL title game.

Under wet conditions, the Chiefs defense dominated Super Bowl IV by limiting the Minnesota offense to only 67 rushing yards, forcing three interceptions, and recovering two fumbles. Kansas City's Len Dawson became the fourth consecutive winning quarterback to be named Super Bowl MVP. He completed 12 of 17 passes for 142 yards and one touchdown, with one interception. Dawson also recorded three rushing attempts for 11 yards.

Super Bowl IV is also notable for NFL Films miking up the Chiefs' Hank Stram during the game, the first time that a head coach had worn a microphone during a Super Bowl.

World Series 1970

Baltimore Orioles

4

Cincinnati Reds

1

The 1970 World Series matched the American League champion Baltimore Orioles (108–54 in the regular season) against the National League champion Cincinnati Reds (102–60), with the Orioles winning in five games.

In this series Emmett Ashford became the first African American to umpire in the Fall Classic. It also featured the first World Series games to be played on artificial turf, as Games 1 and 2 took place at Cincinnati's first-year Riverfront Stadium.

This was the last World Series in which all games were played in the afternoon. Also this was the third time in a World Series where a team leading 3–0 in the series would fail to complete the sweep by losing game 4 but still win game 5 to win the series. 1910 and 1937 were the others. This was the last World Series until 2017 in which both participating teams won over 100 games during the regular season.

Coming into the World Series, the Orioles had won 14 straight including the final 11 during the regular season then defeated the Minnesota Twins, three games to none, in the American League Championship Series for the second straight year. The Reds went 32–30 in their last 62 regular season games, but swept the Pittsburgh Pirates, three games to none, in the National League Championship Series.

The World Series set up to as a classic matchup of a pair of teams laden with all-star players.

Game	Date	Score	Location	Time	Attendance
1	October 10	**Baltimore Orioles** – 4, Cincinnati Reds – 3	Riverfront Stadium	2:24	51,531
2	October 11	**Baltimore Orioles** – 6, Cincinnati Reds – 5	Riverfront Stadium	2:26	51,531
3	October 13	Cincinnati Reds – 3, **Baltimore Orioles** – 9	Memorial Stadium	2:09	51,773
4	October 14	**Cincinnati Reds** – 6, Baltimore Orioles – 5	Memorial Stadium	2:26	53,007
5	October 15	Cincinnati Reds – 3, **Baltimore Orioles** – 9	Memorial Stadium	2:35	45,341

1970 NBA Finals

New York Knicks

4

Los Angeles Lakers

3

The 1970 NBA World Championship Series was the championship series of the 1970 NBA Playoffs, which concluded the 1969–70 National Basketball Association (NBA) season. The Eastern Division champion New York Knicks defeated the Western Division champion Los Angeles Lakers in a best-of-seven series 4 games to 3 for their first NBA title

The final game of the series was named by ESPN in 2010 as the greatest Game 7 in finals history, featuring a return from injury for Willis Reed. Reed's most famous performance took place on May 8, 1970 in Game 7 played at Madison Square Garden. Due to a severe thigh injury suffered in Game 5, a torn muscle that kept him out of Game 6, he was considered unlikely to play in Game 7. Yet Reed surprised the fans by walking onto the court during warmups, prompting widespread applause. Starting the game, he scored the Knicks' first two field goals on his first two shot attempts, his only points of the game. He then played defense on Wilt Chamberlain, limiting him to two shots made in nine attempts. When Reed left for good with 3:05 left in the first half, the Knicks led 61-37. Walt "Clyde" Frazier took it from there, finishing with 36 points and 19 assists as the Knicks won the championship, 113-99. Following the game in the winner's locker room, a moved Howard Cosell told Reed on national television, "You exemplify the very best that the human spirit can offer."

Game	Home Team	Score	Road Team
Game 1	**New York Knicks**	124–112 (1–0)	Los Angeles Lakers
Game 2	New York Knicks	103–105 (1–1)	**Los Angeles Lakers**
Game 3	Los Angeles Lakers	108–112 OT (1–2)	**New York Knicks**
Game 4	**Los Angeles Lakers**	121–115 OT (2–2)	New York Knicks
Game 5	**New York Knicks**	107–100 (3–2)	Los Angeles Lakers
Game 6	**Los Angeles Lakers**	135–113 (3–3)	New York Knicks
Game 7	**New York Knicks**	113–99 (4–3)	Los Angeles Lakers

Knicks win series 4–3

St. Louis Blues

0

Boston Bruins

4

The 1970 Stanley Cup Finals was the championship series of the National Hockey League's (NHL) 1969–70 seasons and the culmination of the 1970 Stanley Cup playoffs.

It was contested between the Boston Bruins and the St. Louis Blues, who appeared in their third straight finals.

The Bruins were making their first appearance in the finals since 1958. The Bruins won the series, four games to none, their first Stanley Cup victory in 29 years. Bobby Orr scored the Cup-winning goal on Glenn Hall, with an assist from Derek Sanderson, at forty seconds of overtime, and the subsequent image of Orr flying through the air, his arms raised in victory — he had been tripped by Blues' defenseman Noel Picard immediately after scoring the goal — is one of the most famous and recognized hockey images of all time. With the win, the Bruins became the first American team to win the Stanley Cup since the Chicago Blackhawks in 1961.

The Blues, who had gone to the Finals in their first three years but lost each time in four-game sweeps, did not appear in the Stanley Cup Finals again until 2019, ending the second longest Finals drought in league history.

May 3	**Boston Bruins**	6–1	St. Louis Blues	St. Louis Arena
May 5	**Boston Bruins**	6–2	St. Louis Blues	St. Louis Arena
May 7	St. Louis Blues	1–4	**Boston Bruins**	Boston Garden
May 10	St. Louis Blues	3–4 OT	**Boston Bruins**	Boston Garden

Boston Bruins win series 4-0

1970 US Open Golf

The 1970 U.S. Open was the 70th U.S. Open, held June 18–21 at Hazeltine National Golf Club in Chaska, Minnesota, a suburb southwest of Minneapolis. Tony Jacklin shot under-par in all four rounds on his way to a seven-stroke victory and his only U.S. Open title, the second of his two major championships. He was the first champion born in England since Cyril Walker in 1924.

Tony Jacklin led wire-to-wire and was hardly threatened throughout the championship. He took a four-shot lead over Dave Hill into the final round, and despite bogeys at the 7th and 8th, made a long birdie putt at 9 to quell any talk of a collapse. Tony Jacklin shot a third consecutive round of 70 and a 281 total, seven clear of the field and the only player under par.

Opened eight years earlier, Hazeltine was hosting its first men's major championship, and reviews were less than positive. Runner-up Hill, when asked what the course lacked, said: "Eighty acres of corn and a few cows. They ruined a good farm when they built this course." The course underwent significant renovations; when the U.S. Open returned twenty-one years later in 1991 it drew generally positive reviews, even from Hill. Hazeltine later hosted the PGA Championship twice (2002, 2009) and the Ryder Cup in 2016.

Tony Jacklin's win was the first in the U.S. Open by a European in over forty years and the last for forty more, until Graeme McDowell won at Pebble Beach in 2010. The next win by an Englishman was three years later in 2013, Justin Rose at Merion.

Place	Player	Country	Score	To par	Money ($)
1	**Tony Jacklin**	England	71-70-70-70=281	−7	30,000
2	Dave Hill	United States	75-69-71-73=288	E	15,000
T3	Bob Charles	New Zealand	76-71-75-67=289	+1	9,000
	Bob Lunn	United States	77-72-70-70=289		
5	Ken Still	United States	78-71-71-71=291	+3	7,000
6	Miller Barber	United States	75-75-72-70=292	+4	6,000
7	Gay Brewer	United States	75-71-71-76=293	+5	5,000
T8	Billy Casper	United States	75-75-71-73=294	+6	3,325
	Bruce Devlin	Australia	75-75-71-73=294		
	Lee Trevino	United States	77-73-74-70=294		
	Larry Ziegler	United States	75-73-73-73=294		

1970 Kentucky Derby

The 1970 Kentucky Derby was the 96th running of the Kentucky Derby. The race took place on May 2, 1970. The race is most notable in American popular culture as the setting for "The Kentucky Derby Is Decadent and Depraved", an article written for Scanlan's Monthly by Hunter S. Thompson that would later be identified as the first instance of gonzo journalism.

Finished	Post	Horse	Jockey	Trainer
1st	3	Dust Commander	Mike Manganello	Don Combs
2nd	7	My Dad George	Ray Broussard	Frank J. McManus
3rd	1	High Echelon	Larry Adams	John W. Jacobs

1970 Preakness Stakes

The 1970 Preakness Stakes was the 95th running of the $205,000 Preakness Stakes thoroughbred horse race. The race took place on May 16, 1970, and was televised in the United States on the CBS television network. Personality, who was jockeyed by Eddie Belmonte, won the race by a scant neck over runner-up My Dad George. Approximate post time was 5:42 p.m. Eastern Time. The race was run on a fast track in a final time of 1:56-1/5. The Maryland Jockey Club reported total attendance of 42,474; this is recorded as third highest on the list of American thoroughbred racing top attended events for North America in 1970.

Finish Position	Margin (lengths)	Post Position	Horse name	Jockey	Trainer
1st	0	1A	Personality	Ethel D. Jacobs	John W. Jacobs
2nd	neck	6	My Dad George	Ray Broussard	Frank J. McManus
3rd	31/4	2	Silent Screen	John L. Rotz	J. Bowes Bond

1970 Belmont Stakes

The Belmont Stakes is an American Grade I stakes Thoroughbred horse race held on the first or second Saturday in June at Belmont Park in Elmont, New York. Belmont Park is known as "The Championship Track" because nearly every major American champion in racing history has competed on the racetrack. Belmont Park, with its wide, sweeping turns and long homestretch, is considered one of the fairest racetracks. It is a 1.5-mile-long (2.4 km) horse race, open to three-year-old Thoroughbreds.

Finished	Post	Horse	Jockey	Trainer
1st	3	High Echelon	John L. Rotz	John W. Jacobs

The Triple Crown

The Triple Crown of Thoroughbred Racing, commonly known as the Triple Crown, is a title awarded to a three-year-old Thoroughbred horse who wins the Kentucky Derby, Preakness Stakes, and Belmont Stakes. The three races were inaugurated in different years, the last being the Kentucky Derby in 1875. These races are now run annually in May and early June of each year. The Triple Crown Trophy, commissioned in 1950 but awarded to all previous winners as well as those after 1950, is awarded to a Triple Crown winner.

World Heavyweight title 1970

On February 16, 1970, Frazier faced WBA Champion Jimmy Ellis at Madison Square Garden. Ellis had outpointed Jerry Quarry in the final bout of the WBA elimination tournament for Ali's vacated belt. Frazier had himself declined to participate in the WBA tournament to protest their decision to strip Ali. Ellis held an impressive win over Oscar Bonavena among others. Beforehand, Ali had announced his retirement and relinquished the Heavyweight title, allowing Ellis and Frazier to fight for the undisputed title. Frazier won by a TKO when Ellis's trainer Angelo Dundee would not let him come out for the 5th round following two 4th round knockdowns (the first knockdowns of Ellis's career). Frazier's decisive win over Ellis was a frightening display of power and tenacity.

In his first title defense, Frazier traveled to Detroit to fight World Light Heavyweight Champion Bob Foster, who would go on to set a record for the number of title defenses in the light-heavyweight division. Frazier (26–0) retained his title by twice flooring the hard punching Foster in the second round. The second knock down came on a devastating left hook and Foster could not beat the count. Then came what was hyped as the "Fight Of The Century," his first fight with Muhammad Ali, who had launched a comeback in 1970 after a three-year suspension from boxing. This would be the first meeting of two undefeated heavyweight champions (and last until Mike Tyson faced Michael Spinks in 1988), since Ali (31–0) had not lost his title in the ring, but rather been stripped because of his refusal to be conscripted into the armed forces, some considered him to be the true champion. This fight was to crown the one, true heavyweight champion.

Joe Frazier

Jimmy Ellis

1970 Indianapolis 500

The 54th 500 Mile International Sweepstakes was held at the Indianapolis Motor Speedway in Speedway, Indiana on Saturday, May 30, 1970.

Al Unser, Sr. dominated the race, winning the pole position and leading 190 laps en route to victory. He joined his brother Bobby as the first duo of brothers to win the Indianapolis 500. It was the first of four victories for Al at Indianapolis. Car owner Parnelli Jones, who won the race as a driver in 1963, became the second individual (after Pete DePaolo) to win separately as both a driver and as an owner.

Unser took home $271,697 out of a record $1,000,002 purse. For the first time in Indy history, the total prize fund topped $1 million.

Rain on race morning delayed the start by about thirty minutes. On the pace lap, Jim Malloy smacked the outside wall in turn four, which delayed the start further.

All 33 cars in the field were turbocharged for the first time. This would be the final 500 in which the winner celebrated in the old victory lane at the south end of the pits. Victory lane would be relocated for 1971.

24 Hour Daytona 1970

The 1970 24 Hours of Daytona was an endurance race at the 3.8 mile road circuit at the Daytona International Speedway, Daytona Beach, Florida, USA that took place on January 31 and February 1, 1970. It was the first race of the 1970 World Sports car Championship season. This was the first race for the iconic Porsche 917K and Ferrari 512S cars.

On the awesome 31-degree high banking of the Daytona Speedway, ex-Aston Martin race team manager John Wyer's Gulf-sponsored team finished 1-2 in the race and broke the distance record by 190 miles; with the #28 works Ferrari finishing 3rd.

Pos	No	Team	Drivers	Chassis	Laps
1	2	🇬🇧 John Wyer Automotive Engineering	🇲🇽 Pedro Rodriguez 🇫🇮 Leo Kinnunen 🇬🇧 Brian Redman	Porsche 917K	724
2	1	🇬🇧 John Wyer Automotive Engineering	🇨🇭 Jo Siffert 🇬🇧 Brian Redman	Porsche 917K	679
3	28	🇮🇹 SpA Ferrari SEFAC	🇺🇸 Mario Andretti 🇮🇹 Arturo Merzario 🇧🇪 Jacky Ickx	Ferrari 512S	676

BOOK PUBLICATIONS

Bury My Heart at Wounded Knee: An Indian History of the American West is a 1970 book by American writer Dee Brown that covers the history of Native Americans in the American West in the late nineteenth century. The book expresses details of the history of American expansionism from a point of view that is critical of its effects on the Native Americans. Brown describes Native Americans' displacement through forced relocations and years of warfare waged by the United States federal government. The government's dealings are portrayed as a continuing effort to destroy the culture, religion, and way of life of Native American peoples. Helen Hunt Jackson's A Century of Dishonor is often considered a nineteenth-century precursor to Dee Brown's writing.

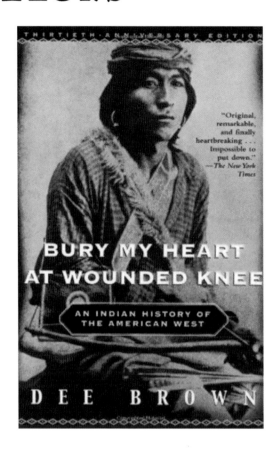

In the first chapter, Brown presents a brief history of the discovery and settlement of America, from 1492 to the Indian turmoil that began in 1860. He stresses the initially gentle and peaceable behavior of Indians toward Europeans, especially given their apparent lack of resistance to early colonial efforts at Europeanization. It was not until the further influx of European settlers, gradual encroachment, and eventual seizure of American lands by the "white man" that the Native people were shown to exhibit forms of major resistance

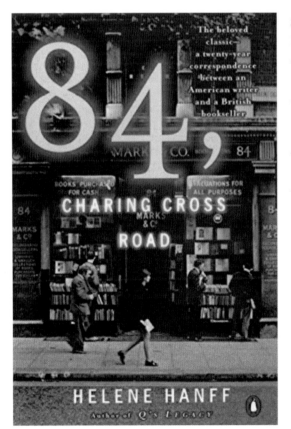

84, Charing Cross Road is a 1970 book by Helene Hanff, later made into a stage play, television play, and film, about the twenty-year correspondence between the author and Frank Doel, chief buyer of Marks & Co antiquarian booksellers, located at the eponymous address in London, England.

Helene Hanff was in search of obscure classics and British literature titles that she had been unable to find in New York City when she noticed an ad in the Saturday Review of Literature. She first contacted the shop in 1949 and it fell to Doel to fulfil her requests. In time, a long-distance friendship developed between the two and between Hanff and other staff members, as well, with an exchange of Christmas packages, birthday gifts and food parcels to help with the post-World War II food shortages in Britain. Their letters included discussions about topics as diverse as the sermons of John Donne, how to make Yorkshire Pudding, the Brooklyn Dodgers and the coronation of Elizabeth II. Hanff postponed visiting her English friends until too late; Doel died in December 1968 from peritonitis from a burst appendix, and the bookshop eventually closed in December 1970. Hanff did finally visit Charing Cross Road and the empty shop in the summer of 1971, a trip recorded in her 1973 book The Duchess of Bloomsbury Street.

The Crystal Cave is a 1970 fantasy novel by Mary Stewart. The first in a quintet of novels covering the Arthurian legend.

This novel covers the time from Merlin's sixth year until he becomes a young man. The Romans have recently left Britain, which is now divided into a number of kingdoms loosely united under a High King. Merlin is the illegitimate son of a Welsh princess, who refuses to name his father. Small for his age and often abused or neglected, Merlin occasionally has clairvoyant visions. These visions and his unknown parentage cause him to be referred to as "the son of a devil" and "bastard child". Educated by a hermit, Galapas, who teaches him to use his psychic powers as well as his earthly gifts, Merlin eventually finds his way to the court of Ambrosius Aurelianus in Brittany. There, he assists in Ambrosius's preparations to invade and unify Britain, defeat Vortigern and his Saxon allies, and become its High King. Also exiled in Brittany is Uther, Ambrosius's brother, heir and supporter. It is revealed that Merlin is Ambrosius's son, the result of a brief relationship between Ambrosius and Merlin's mother.

Merlin returns to Britain but finds Galapas killed. He is captured by Vortigern who is attempting to build a fortress at Dinas Emrys - but each night the newly built walls collapse.

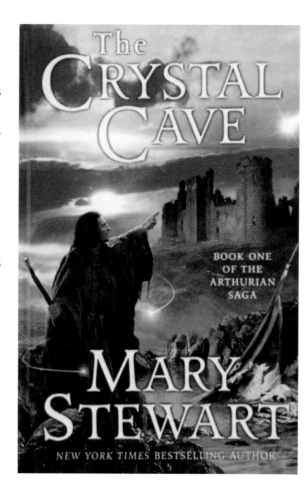

The Bluest Eye, published in 1970, was the first novel written by author Toni Morrison. Morrison was an African-American novelist, a Pulitzer and Nobel Prize winner whose works are praised for addressing the harsh consequences of racism in the United States.

The novel takes place in Lorain, Ohio (Morrison's own home town), and tells the story of a young African-American lady named Pecola who grows up during the years following the Great Depression. Set in 1941, the story tells that due to her mannerisms and dark skin, she is consistently regarded as "ugly". As a result, she develops an inferiority complex, which fuels her desire for the blue eyes she equates with "whiteness".

The point of view of the novel switches between various perspectives of Claudia MacTeer, the daughter of Pecola's foster parents, at different stages in her life. In addition, there is an omniscient third-person narrative which includes inset narratives in the first person.

Due to its controversial topics of racism, incest, and child molestation, there have been numerous attempts to ban the novel from schools and libraries.

Fantastic Mr. Fox is a children's novel written by British author Roald Dahl. It was published in 1970, by George Allen & Unwin in the UK and Alfred A. Knopf in the U.S., with illustrations by Donald Chaffin. The first U.K. Puffin paperback, first issued in 1974, featured illustrations by Jill Bennett. Later editions have featured illustrations by Tony Ross (1988) and Quentin Blake (1996). The story is about Mr. Fox and how he outwits his farmer neighbors to steal their food from right under their noses. In 2009, it was adapted into a film by Wes Anderson.

The story revolves around an anthropomorphic, tricky, and clever fox named Mr. Fox who lives underground beside a tree with his wife and four children. In order to feed his family, he makes night visits to farms owned by three wicked, rude, cruel and dim-witted farmers named Boggis, Bunce and Bean and snatches away the livestock available on each man's farm. Tired of being outsmarted by Mr. Fox, the farmers devise a plan to ambush him as he leaves his burrow, but they succeed only in shooting off his tail. The farmers then dig up the Foxes' burrow using spades and then excavators. The Foxes manage to escape by burrowing further beneath the earth to safety. The trios of farmers are ridiculed for their persistence but they refuse to give up and vow not to return to their farms until they have caught Mr. Fox.

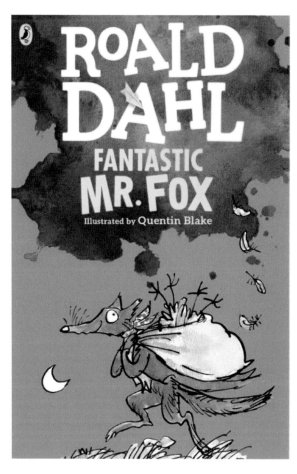

The Driver's Seat is a novella by Muriel Spark. Published in 1970, it was advertised as "a metaphysical shocker". It is indeed in the psychological thriller genre, dealing with themes of alienation, isolation and loss of spiritual values.

Lise is a spinster, working in an accountancy firm somewhere in Northern Europe, probably Denmark (the location is not explicitly specified). Spark described The Driver's Seat as a 'whydunnit' (and she uses the term in the novel). This is because in the novel's third chapter it is revealed that Lise will be murdered. Hence Spark's novel is an examination, not of what events take place, but why they do.

It is eventually revealed that Lise has suffered years of illness; she behaves erratically and often confrontationally, and wears garish, provocative clothing. Lise travels to a South European city, probably Rome, ostensibly to meet her illusory boyfriend.

It was filmed in 1974 starring Elizabeth Taylor and featuring Andy Warhol. In the U.S the film was renamed Identikit. Spark described it as one of her favorite novels. In 2015, it was adapted for the stage for the first time by Laurie Sansom for a National Theatre of Scotland production which premiered at the Royal Lyceum Theatre, Edinburgh.

Troubles. A 1970 novel by J. G. Farrell. The novel concerns the arrival of Englishman Major Brendan Archer, recently discharged from the British Army, at the Majestic Hotel on the Wexford coast in south-east Ireland in 1919. Both the hotel, and the town in which it is situated, Kilnalough, are fictional. Archer is convinced he is engaged, though sure he had never actually proposed, to Angela Spencer, the daughter of Edward Spencer, the elderly owner of the hotel. She has written to him since they met in 1916 while on leave from the trench warfare of the Western Front.

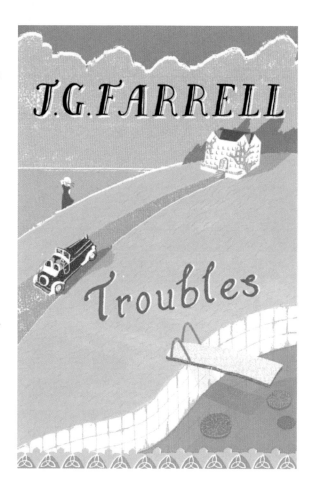

The Spencer's are an Anglo-Irish Protestant family, strongly Unionist in their attitudes towards Ireland's ties to the United Kingdom. Archer functions as a confused observer of the dysfunctional Spencer family, representing the Anglo-Irish, and the local Catholic population. As the novel progresses, social and economic relationships break down, mirrored by the gentle decay of the hotel. While the Irish War of Independence forms the background to the events of the novel, the political upheaval is not treated as a theme. Apart from occasional news reports concerning the war, the only references to it are chance remarks from the novel's characters. The novel's action takes place mostly within the hotel, with the remainder of the scenes taking place almost entirely in the surrounding areas.

Time and Again is a 1970 illustrated novel by American writer Jack Finney. The many illustrations in the book are real, though, as explained in an endnote, not all are from the 1882 period in which the actions of the book take place.

In November 1970, Simon Morley, an advertising sketch artist, is approached by U.S. Army Major Ruben Prien to participate in a secret government project. He is taken to a huge warehouse on the West Side of Manhattan, where he views what seem to be movie sets, with people acting on them. It seems this is a project to learn whether it is feasible to send people back into the past by what amounts to self-hypnosis—whether, by convincing oneself that one is in the past, not the present, one can make it so. As it turns out, Simon (usually called Si) has a good reason to want to go back to the past—his girlfriend, Kate, has a mystery linked to New York City in 1882. She has a letter dated from that year, mailed to an Andrew Carmody (a fictional minor figure who was associated with Grover Cleveland). The letter seems innocuous enough—a request for a meeting to discuss marble—but there is a note which, though half burned, seems to say that the sending of the letter led to "the destruction by fire of the entire World", followed by a missing word. Carmody, the writer of the note, mentioned his blame for that incident. He then killed himself.

Love Story is a 1970 romance novel by American writer Erich Segal. Love Story is romantic and funny, yet tragic. It is the tale of two college students whose love enables them to overcome the adversities they encounter in life: Oliver Barrett IV, a Harvard jock and heir to the Barrett fortune and legacy, and Jennifer Cavilleri, the quick-witted daughter of a Rhode Island baker. Oliver (Ollie) was expected to assume control of his father's business empire, while Jennifer (Jenny) was a music major studying at Radcliffe College and planning to study in Paris. From very different worlds, Oliver and Jenny are immediately attracted to each other and their love deepens.

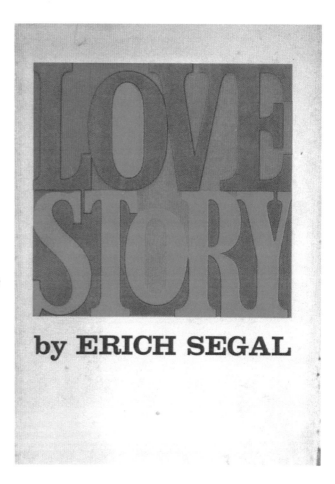

by ERICH SEGAL

The story of Jenny and Ollie is a story of two young people who come from two separate worlds and are brought together in the unlikeliest of ways. Upon graduation from college, the two decide to marry, against the wishes of Oliver's father, who promptly severs all ties with his son. Without financial support, the couple struggles to pay Oliver's way through Harvard's Law School, with Jenny working as a private school teacher. Graduating third in his class, Oliver gets several job offers and takes up a position at a respectable New York law firm.

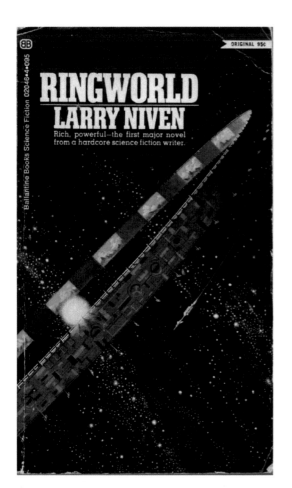

Ringworld is a 1970 science fiction novel by Larry Niven. On planet Earth in 2850 AD, Louis Gridley Wu is celebrating his 200th birthday. Despite his age, Louis is in perfect physical condition (due to the longevity drug boosterspice). He has once again become bored with human society and is thinking about taking one of his periodic sabbaticals, alone in a spaceship far away from other people. He meets Nessus, a Pierson's puppeteer, who offers him a mysterious job. Intrigued, Louis eventually accepts. Speaker-to-Animals (Speaker), who is a Kzin, and Teela Brown, a young human woman who becomes Louis' lover, also join the crew. They first go to the puppeteer home world, where they learn that the expedition's goal is to investigate the Ringworld, a gigantic artificial ring, to see if it poses any threat. The Ringworld is about one million miles (1.6 million km) wide and approximately the diameter of Earth's orbit (which makes it about 600 million miles or 950 million km in circumference), encircling a sun like star. It rotates to provide artificial gravity 99.2% as strong as Earth's from centrifugal force. The Ringworld has a habitable, flat inner surface (equivalent in area to approximately three million Earths), a breathable atmosphere and a temperature optimal for humans. Night is provided by an inner ring of shadow squares which are connected to each other by thin, ultra-strong wire. When the crew completes their mission, they will be given the starship in which they travelled to the puppeteer home world.

1970 OSCAR WINNERS

BEST ACTOR

John Wayne   True Grit

BEST ACTRESS

Maggie Smith   The Prime of Miss Jean Brodie

BEST DIRECTOR

John Schlesinger   Midnight Cowboy

BEST MOTION PICTURE

Midnight Cowboy   Jerome Hellman

BEST SUPPORTING ACTOR

Gig Young   They Shoot Horses, Don't They?

BEST SUPPORTING ACTRESS

Goldie Hawn   Cactus Flower

BEST STORY AND SCREENPLAY

Butch Cassidy and the Sundance Kid   William Goldman

BEST MUSIC SCORE

Butch Cassidy and the Sundance Kid   Burt Bacharach

BEST SCORING OF A MUSICAL PICTURE BEST SONG

Hello, Dolly !   Lennie Hayton and Lionel Newman

BEST SONG

Raindrops Keep Fallin' On My Head   Butch Cassidy and the Sundance Kid

BEST SOUND

Hello, Dolly !   Jack Solomon, Murray Spivack

BEST CINEMATOGRAPHY

Butch Cassidy and the Sundance Kid   Conrad Hall

BEST SPECIAL EFFECTS

Marooned   Robbie Robertson

The 42nd Academy Awards were presented April 7, 1970, at the Dorothy Chandler Pavilion in Los Angeles, California. For the second year in a row, there was no official host. This was the first Academy Awards ceremony to be broadcast via satellite to an international audience, but only outside North America. Mexico and Brazil were the sole countries to broadcast the event live.

This is currently the highest rated of the televised Academy Awards ceremonies, according to Nielsen ratings. The record, as of 2019, remains unbroken thanks to the emergence of the Super Bowl as the biggest annual event of awards season.

Midnight Cowboy became the first – and so far, the only – X-rated film to win the Academy Award for Best Picture. Its rating has since been downgraded to R. The previous year had seen the only G-rated film to win Best Picture, Carol Reed's Oliver!

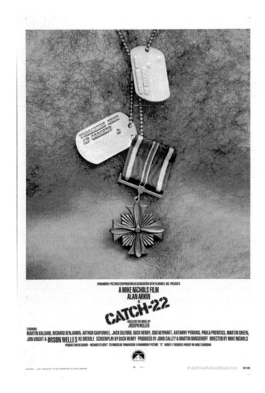

Catch 22. WW2, the Mediterranean theatre. Captain Yossarian is the bombardier of a B-25 medium bomber. His squadron's missions largely involve bombing targets on the Italian mainland.

A veteran of countless missions, he has become cynical about the war and pessimistic about his chances of surviving. He should have been rotated home a long time ago, but the Wing's Commanding Officer, Colonel Cathcart, keeps raising the number of missions required to rotate out.

Yossarian hits upon a plan to get sent home. However, there's a catch.

Nominated for best Cinematography

The film cost around 18 million dollars to make and returned $24,911,670 at the box office.

Trivia

Second Unit Director John Jordan refused to wear a harness during a bomber scene. While giving a hand signal to another airplane from the tail gunner position in the camera plane, he lost his grip and fell four thousand feet to his death.

Director Mike Nichols wanted thirty-six B-25s to create the big U.S. Army Air Forces base, but the budget couldn't stretch to more than seventeen flyable Mitchells. An additional non-flyable hulk was acquired in Mexico, made barely ferry-able and flown with landing gear down to location, only to be burned and destroyed in the landing crash scene. The wreck was then buried in the ground next to the runway, where it remains to this day.

While on a tirade in his office, Major (Bob Newhart) walks past a framed photo of Franklin D. Roosevelt. In a continuous shot, he paces around his office, and when he passes the picture again, it is of Winston Churchill, as he makes one more round of his office and grabs the fake moustache out of his filing cabinet, the photo has changed to that of Joseph Stalin.

Goofs

In Major Danby's initial scene in the control tower, the Baby Ruth bar in his pocket is in a modern (1970) wrapper. The actual 1940s wrappers had a different design.

When the chaplain is stopped by Milo on his way to talk with Cathcart his jacket is covered in light colored dirt spots. They are gone when he arrives at the top of the stairs and starts talking to Orr.

When 1st Lt. Milo Minderbinder explains to Cathcart his plans to trade blankets to the Italians for fresh eggs, he shows Cathcart an egg. As the two walk along the landing strip, the egg disappears from Milo's hand.

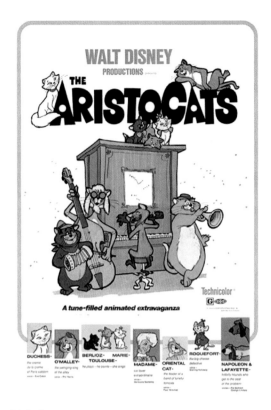

The Aristocats. Retired Madame Adelaide Bonfamille enjoys the good life in her Paris villa with even classier cat Duchess and three kittens: pianist Berlioz, painter Toulouse and sanctimonious Marie.

When loyal butler Edgar overhears her will leaves everything to the cats until their death, he drugs and kidnaps them. However retired army dogs make his sidecar capsize on the country.

Crafty stray cat Thomas O'Malley takes them under his wing back to Paris. Edgar tries to cover his tracks and catch them at return, but more animals turn on him, from the cart horse Frou-Frou to the tame mouse Roquefort and O'Malley's jazz friends.

The film cost around $4,000,000 to produce and in the first weekend alone made $3,200,200.

In total the film made $37,675,257 at the box office.

Trivia

This was the last animated feature to be approved by Walt Disney and the studio's first animated feature to be entirely completed after his death. It should be noted, however, that Disney had spent time working on the story for Les aventures de Bernard et Bianca (1977) (released seven years later) around the time The Jungle Book (1967) entered production.

The character of Scat Cat was designed to be voiced by Louis Armstrong. The character's look was modelled after Armstrong - the way he played his trumpet, his roly-poly physique, and right down to the prominent gap between his teeth. However, Armstrong was unable to record a single line due to illness. His replacement, Scatman Crothers, was directed to "Pretend you're Satchmo."

The dogs Napoleon and Lafayette are both named after famous French generals Napoléon Bonaparte and Marquis De Lafayette. Napoleon was the emperor of France who conquered much of Europe. Lafayette was a nobleman who helped the Americans during the American Revolution.

Goofs

Traffic lights are shown during Edgar's drive through Paris with the cats. Apart from a traffic light installed in 1868 (which exploded in 1869) in London outside the Houses of Parliament, traffic lights were first used in 1914 in Cleveland, Ohio, four years after this movie takes place. (with three-color traffic lights first used in Detroit in 1920.)

The truck at the end of the film is a Morris-Commercial FE Series, which wasn't made until 1955, which was 45 years after the film is set, and 15 years before the film was released.

When Marie hops up onto the piano, the lowest keys are hit, but the sounds come from keys in a much higher register. The same thing happens when Berlioz slides down the keyboard to get back at Marie for pulling him off the bench; the keys sound much higher than they should.

M*A*S*H. The personnel at the 4077 MASH unit deal with the horrors of the Korean War and the stresses faced in surgery by whatever means. The tone at the MASH is established by recent arrivals, surgeons Captains 'Hawkeye' Pierce, 'Duke' Forrest, and 'Trapper' John McIntyre - the latter who Hawkeye knows he's met somewhere, but Trapper who won't divulge where - whose antics can be best described as non-regulation, and in the negative words of one of their fellow MASH-ers: unmilitary.

The unit's commanding officer, Colonel Henry Blake, doesn't care about this behavior as long as it doesn't affect him, and as long as they do their job and do it well, which they do. Their behavior does extremely bother fellow surgeon, Major Frank Burns, and recently arrived head nurse, Major Margaret Houlihan, who obtains the nickname 'Hot Lips' based on information they glean about her through underhanded means. Beyond their battles with Frank and Hot Lips, Hawkeye, Duke and/or Trapper help unit dentist Painless.

Oscar winner for Best Writing, Screenplay Based on Material from Another Medium.
Also nominees for Best Picture, Best Actress in a supporting Role, Best Director and Best Film Editing.

Trivia

The fourteen-year-old son of director Robert Altman, Mike, wrote the lyrics to the theme song "Suicide is Painless". Because of its inclusion in the subsequent television series, he continued to get residuals throughout its run and syndication. His father was paid $75,000 for directing, but his son eventually made about $2 million in song royalties.

The first take of the shot where Hot Lips is revealed in the shower didn't work because Sally Kellerman anticipated the reveal, and was already lying on the floor when the tent flap went up. To distract her, Robert Altman and Gary Burghoff entered the shower tent and dropped their trousers while the shot was rolling outside. While Kellerman was staring at them, the tent flap was raised, resulting in her genuine surprise and shock when she realized what had happened. In the Special Edition double disc DVD, they say that Radar is standing naked beside the camera, and that's the reason why Sally Kellerman looks so surprised when the flap was raised.

Goofs

The football helmets worn in the game are of late 1960s vintage, with the familiar "modern" round shape and face masks. A football game during the Korean War would have likely featured early-model plastic helmets shaped like the older leather-style helmets with no face masks.

Trapper John (Elliott Gould) was not only not dressed or groomed within the regulations of the US Army of the 1950's, it wasn't acceptable during the 1970s filming of movie. There's no way that a military officer (doctor or not) would be allowed to report to a military unit looking as he did.

When Hot Lips confronts Lt. Col. Blake after she was exposed in the shower, she stands framed in the doorway of Lt. Col. Blake's tent. To her left, there is a mirror hanging on the tent wall that appears/disappears between shots.

"THE EPIC AMERICAN WAR MOVIE THAT HOLLYWOOD HAS ALWAYS WANTED TO MAKE BUT NEVER HAD THE GUTS TO DO BEFORE."
- Vincent Canby, New York Times

"YOU MAY NEVER HAVE ANOTHER EXPERIENCE LIKE IT! EVIDENTLY SOMEONE BELIEVED THAT THE PUBLIC HAD COME OF AGE ENOUGH TO TAKE A MATURE FILM ABOUT A REAL WAR WITH A HERO-VILLAIN IN ALL HIS GLORIOUS AND VAINGLORIOUS HUMANITY."
- Liz Smith, Cosmopolitan Magazine

Patton. Biopic of the famed - many would say infamous - World War II General George S. Patton, Jr. The story begins in North Africa with his appointment as the commanding general of II Corps soon after their devastating defeat at the hands of Rommel's Afrika Korps at Kasserine Pass.

After leading II Corps during the invasion of Sicily, Patton faced one of his severest tests when, after slapping a hospitalized soldier suffering from battle fatigue, he is reprimanded and forced to publicly apologize. It and other faux pas ultimately leads to Patton being relieved and not being assigned to command again until several months after D-Day where he takes charge of the U.S. Third Army.

Patton is portrayed as a prima donna and a hardened no-nonsense commander whose main objective is always to win - regardless of the cost which in these circumstances was mostly in the form of human lives.

Winner of 7 Oscars for Best Picture, Best Actor, Best Director, Best Writing, Best Art Direction, Best Sound and Best Film Editing.
Also nominated for Best Cinematography, Best Effects and Best Music.

Trivia

Patton's biographer, Carlo D'Este, suggested that his melancholy and increasingly extraordinary behaviour may have been due to brain damage resulting from a series of head injuries caused by a lifetime of falls from horses and road accidents - the most serious being an accident in Hawaii in 1936 that had resulted in a two-day blackout. He concluded, however, that we will never know, for after his death Beatrice refused to allow an autopsy on the body despite a request from the Army.

The ivory-handled revolvers George C. Scott wears in the opening speech were actually George S. Patton's bona-fide revolvers.

The movie begins without showing the 20th Century-Fox logo, or any other indication that the film is starting. At military bases across the US theatre owners reported that soldiers in the audience would often stand up and snap to attention when they heard the movie's opening line ("Ten-hut!"), assuming it to be a real call to attention.

Goofs

The American insignia on the fuselage of the C-47 transport plane carrying Patton and his staff to France is incorrect. It is shown as a white star on a blue circle. In actuality, by 1944 when this event occurred, a large white bar had been added to each side of the circled star. Furthermore, starting on D-Day and for the next several months afterward, all Allied aircraft operating over Normandy were marked with distinctive "Invasion" or "Overlord" stripes, alternating white and black stripes wrapped around the wings and the rear fuselage.

The tanks used in the major battle scene in North Africa are post-war tanks. On the German side the M48 tank (1953) was used and on the American side the M41 Walker Bulldog (1953), M46 Patton (1949) and (mostly) M47 Patton tanks (1952). Ironically, the M46, M47 and M48 were named "Patton."

PARAMOUNT PICTURES PRESENTS

Ali MacGraw · Ryan O'Neal

The Year's #1 Best Seller

A HOWARD G. MINSKY - ARTHUR HILLER Production

John Marley & Ray Milland ERICH SEGAL ARTHUR HILLER

HOWARD G. MINSKY DAVID GOLDEN FRANCIS LAI GP IN COLOR A PARAMOUNT PICTURE

Love Story. The love story of young adults Oliver Barrett IV and Jenny Cavilleri is told. Oliver comes from an extremely well off and old money New England family, the Barrett name which holds much gravitas and which is plastered especially all over Harvard where Oliver is in pre-law. Like those before him, he plans on attending Harvard Law School, which is not an issue in either the school not accepting him or he not wanting to attend. He has an extremely stiff relationship with his parents, especially his father, Oliver Barrett III, who loves his son in the old school way. Jenny, a music student at Radcliffe, comes from a working class Rhode Island background, she working her way through the program before she plans on going to Paris to further her studies. Unlike Oliver's relationship with his father, Jenny has a very casual one with her baker father, who she calls by his given name Phil. When Oliver and Jenny meet, there are immediate fireworks - she always with a quick quip to put him in his place - both of a good and bad kind, but they both quickly come to the realization that they are in love with each other. They have many obstacles to overcome in having a committed relationship, outwardly his father's disapproval of someone like her not being Barrett material being arguably the biggest. However, other things that happen in the natural course of life and death may trump all.

Trivia

The scenes with Oliver walking alone through a snowy New York were added after principal photography was completed. The production was almost out of money and did not have the necessary funds for permits to shoot in New York City again - so all the shots were grabbed "illegally" using a skeleton film crew and Ryan O'Neal.

Film debut of Tommy Lee Jones, a Harvard graduate. Erich Segal based Ryan O'Neal's character on Jones, and on his Harvard roommate, future Vice-President Al Gore.

To prepare for their roles, Ryan O'Neal learned to ice skate and Ali MacGraw learned to play the harpsichord.

The most famous line from the film, "Love means never having to say you're sorry", was actually misspoken from the script. Originally the line was supposed to be: "Love means not ever having to say you're sorry."

Goofs

During the Cornell/Harvard hockey match, before Oliver enters the penalty box, his hockey jersey is almost spotless. After he sits down and takes off his helmet, a large blood smear appears on his jersey near his shoulder.

In the hospital scene towards the end, Jenny's hair on the left side of the pillow keeps changing position every time the camera angle changes, although she herself has presumably not moved.

During Harvard v Dartmouth Oliver is seen wearing #7 jersey for Harvard. In the penalty box he tells Jenny that he is concentrating on how he is going to total the Dartmouth player who had him sent to the box. He points to the Dartmouth player who at this point has just taken down another Harvard player that is clearly wearing #7.

When Oliver talks with Phil at the hospital, his hand suddenly appears on Phil's shoulder.

Kelly's Heroes. During World War II a German Colonel is captured by the Americans but before he can be interrogated an artillery barrage hits the camp. However, Ex-Lieutenant Kelly manages to reach the Colonel, get him drunk and learn that he is on a secret mission to ship $16,000,000 of gold to a base in France.

Kelly is determined to get the gold and plans for himself and a few of his fellow soldiers to slip into enemy territory and steal the bullion.

Kelly's Heroes brilliantly mixes your average war movie with a bank robbery movie to come up with a plot that's entirely unique. Equipped with an all-star cast, Clint Eastwood and Telly Savalas play the straight guys to the comic antics of Donald Sutherland and Don Rickles. The movie makes no moral judgements about bad guys and good guys and simply shows the characters of both sides a path to redemption in the midst of war.

In addition, the theme song, "Burning Bridges" is rendered with a youthful tone by the Mike Curb Congregation, which reminds us that in reality, people not much removed from childhood are the ones sent into battle.

Trivia

Donald Sutherland became seriously ill during filming on location in Yugoslavia. His wife received a telegram telling her to come immediately but warning her that he would probably be dead before she arrived.

It was during shooting in Yugoslavia in 1969 that Donald Sutherland received word, via co-star Clint Eastwood, that his then-wife Shirley Douglas was arrested for trying to buy hand grenades for the Black Panthers with a personal check from an undercover FBI agent. Sutherland recounts this story often, mentioning that when Eastwood got to the part about the personal check he laughed so hard that he fell to his knees, and Sutherland had to help him up. Eastwood then put his arm around Sutherland and walked him down the hill that overlooked the Yugoslav countryside, assuring his friend his complete support of his predicament. Sutherland and Douglas, who are the parents of Kiefer Sutherland and twin sister Rachel Sutherland, divorced in 1970.

The movie was mainly filmed in Yugoslavia because the Yugoslavian army still had a large quantity of Sherman tanks in 1970.

Goofs

The American fighter plane that attacks Kelly's group is actually a Yugoslav "Ikarus Type 522" trainer that flew for the first time in 1955.

When the tank blows the front doors of the bank open and Kelly others are entering the bank, other soldiers are seen running in from a side room of the bank. Where did they come from since presumably there was no other entrances to the bank since tank was needed to blow the front doors open?

Following the retreat from the barn / death of the German Colonel, while the men are resting alongside the convoy, Stuart Margolin's jeep is followed by a Willys M-38 Jeep which wasn't produced until 1950.

Two Mules For Sister Sara. Cynical Secession War veteran Hogan is in Mexico to earn a fortune trading arms to the Juarista rebels against the French troops of emperor Maximilian.

He takes pity, with ever more mixed feelings, on maverick nun Sara, who is pursued by French cavalry.

Godless Hogan never picks up she's ignorant in religious matters, while obviously the contrary in anything profane.

Stuck on the wrong side of Mexican law and facing the semi-hostile Yaqui tribe, they mutually confide and find both to be heading for a French fort to be taken by the Juaristas, whose rustic 'colonel' Beltran only leads a bunch of war-ignorant peasants and requires him to fetch explosives from Texas.

Only after they bond in several adventures, he learns her true crime and identity.

Trivia

The film's title is actually a pun. Sara's initial transportation is a mule, that becomes lame, and she trades it for a younger and smaller donkey - which is not technically a mule. So, the second "mule" of the title may be Hogan, whom Sara says "You're as stubborn as my mule." Later, she calls Hogan, "Mr. Mule".

While in Austria filming Where Eagles Dare (1968), Clint Eastwood was approached with the script by Elizabeth Taylor, Richard Burton's wife at the time, with the notion of starring together in the film. However, Universal Pictures was unwilling to pay Taylor's high salary.

Shirley MacLaine wrote that since this was filmed in Mexico, it took substantial time to send the film to California for processing and return it for dailies. When MacLaine finally saw the dailies, she was appalled at how overstated her false eyelashes looked, as she was playing a hooker posing as a nun. She regretted that she could not remove them for the rest of the filming because the footage would not match.

Goofs

The story takes place during the French intervention in Mexico from 1861 to 1867. Dynamite was invented in 1867 by Nobel, yet it was not easily available in the US until at least 1868. A common error in westerns.

The story takes place during the French intervention in Mexico from 1861 to 1867. Hogan is using a Colt Peacemaker pistol, which did not come into use until 1873. The rifles Winchester 1873, Gras 1874, Bertie 1907, and a revolver Colt New Service 1917 were not in use at the movie epoch.

In the tunnel scenes, Hogan and friends are using hand-held carbide lamps. Carbide was not produced in any quantity until 1892, and carbide lamps were not invented until several years later.

The train locomotive has the headlight mounted in the center of the smokebox door, which was not common practice until the early 1900s.

The Railway Children. The film opens in a happy, comfortable upper middle-class home in Edwardian London. One night in 1905, the three children see their father usher two strangers into his study. After an argument he leaves with them and does not return.

They and their mother fall on hard times and eventually move to a cottage in the country. Yet they keep their spirits up and find ways to help others.

Fascinated by the nearby railway, they wave to the passengers faithfully every day, and their vigilance and courage prevent an accident.

Their kindness makes friends of some important people who can help solve the mystery of their missing father.

The film had two BAFTA Award nominees for Most Promising Newcomer to Leading Film Roles and Best Supporting Actor.

Trivia

Sally Thomsett was 20 when she was cast as 11-year-old Phyllis. Her contract forbade her to reveal her true age during the making of the film and she was not allowed to be seen smoking, drinking, going out with her boyfriend or driving the sports cars that were her passion. Even the film crew did not know her true age.

Lionel Jeffries grounded Jenny Agutter and Sally Thomsett when he caught them in a nightclub in Leeds after they had sneaked off the set for a night on the town.

Producer Lionel Jeffries chose to use the real name Oakworth (the station where most of the film was shot), changing the name from Meadow Vale as used in E. Nesbit's original novel.

The British Film Institute ranks this film as the 66th Best British Film of all time, the only children's film to make the list.

Goofs

The children's' father dresses in the 'traditional' red and white Father Christmas outfit in order to hand out the presents. Father Christmas has a long and rich history, but up until 1931 he had been portrayed most often in black and white, or green and white. It was in 1931, that Coca-Cola created an image of Father Christmas in red and white, for a Christmas advertising campaign. So although theoretically possible, it is unlikely that red and white costumes would have been used in Edwardian England.

When the children run down the meadow towards the railway line (near the end of the film) you can clearly see a white car going along a road towards the top of the screen. This film is set in 1905.

When the family moves to Yorkshire in 1905, the children run through the field and stand at the gate to wave to the train. There is a vapor trail in the sky.

The bizarre world you met in "Planet Of The Apes" was only the beginning...

WHAT LIES BENEATH MAY BE THE END!

An army of civilized apes... A fortress of radiation-crazed super humans... Earth's final battle is about to begin— Beneath the atomic rubble of what was once the city of New York!

Beneath the Planet of the Apes. Brent is an American astronaut, part of a team sent to locate missing fellow American astronaut, George Taylor. Following Taylor's known flight trajectory, the search and rescue team crash lands on an unknown planet much like Earth in the year 3955, with Brent being the only survivor of the team.

What Brent initially does not know, much like Taylor didn't initially know when he landed here before Brent, is that he has landed back on Earth in the future, in the vicinity of what was New York City.

Brent finds evidence that Taylor has been on the planet. In Brent's search for Taylor, he finds that the planet is run by a barbaric race of English speaking apes, whose mission is in part to annihilate the human race. Brent eventually locates some of those humans, who communicate telepathically and who live underground to prevent detection by the apes.

The film cost $3,000,000 to produce and the box office returned $18,999,817.

Trivia

The only film in the original series of five that do not star Roddy McDowall, because he was committed to another project. Archive footage of McDowall as Cornelius is played at the start, and David Watson plays the character in the film proper. Despite this, McDowall is often pictured on video and DVD packaging for this film.

Despite the original being a significant success, the budget was slashed for this sequel. It went from five million dollars to 2.5 million dollars in one fell swoop. This was mainly due to 20th Century Fox teetering on the brink of bankruptcy following some majorly expensive failures, such as Hello, Dolly! (1969) Star! (1968) and Tora! Tora! Tora! (1970) The recruiting of Ted Post as director was instrumental here as he was used to minimal budgets and shortened schedules from his work on television.

Orson Welles was offered the role of General Ursus, which he turned down. Burt Reynolds was considered for the lead role of John Brent, before James Franciscus was cast due to his resemblance to Charlton Heston. Don Medford agreed to direct the movie, but walked out after the budget was halved.

Goofs

When Taylor looks back at the ship's clock for Earth in Planet of the Apes, it reads November 25, 3978. However, Brent tells his dying commander that the year is 3955. This is repeated in Escape from the Planet of the Apes.

During the prison-cell fight between Taylor & Brent, you can clearly see during certain shots that Brent's double does not have a beard. It then cuts to Brent (James Franciscus) who most definitely does have a beard, as evidenced through the entire movie.

When Brent changes clothes behind the bush, he is wearing boxers. After the horse is shot and he falls along the hillside, he is obviously wearing briefs.

When Brent and Nova are running along the hillside after the horse is shot, his arm bandage clearly falls off, but in the next shot which is closer, it's back on again.

The Private life of Sherlock Holmes. Director Billy Wilder adds a new and intriguing twist to the personality of intrepid detective Sherlock Holmes.

One thing hasn't changed however: Holmes' crime-solving talents. Holmes and Dr. Watson take on the case of a beautiful woman whose husband has vanished. The investigation proves strange indeed, involving six missing midgets, villainous monks, a Scottish castle, the Loch Ness monster, and covert naval experiments.

Can the sleuths make sense of all this and solve the mystery? Originally, the scenes featuring the Loch Ness Monster were intended to be filmed in the actual Loch.

A life size prop was built which had several Nessie like humps which were used to disguise the flotation devices.

The humps were removed, however, at Billy Wilder's request during a test run in the Loch the monster prop sank and was never recovered.

Trivia

Originally, the scenes featuring the Loch Ness Monster were intended to be filmed in the actual Loch. A life-size prop was built which had several Nessie-like humps used to disguise flotation devices. The humps were removed, however, at Billy Wilder's request. Unfortunately, during a test run in Loch Ness, the Monster-prop sank and was never recovered. A second prop, a miniature with just the head and neck, was built, but was only filmed inside a studio tank. Geneviève Page said of this in the biography "Nobody's Perfect: Billy Wilder" by Charlotte Chandler): "When we lost our Loch Ness monster, he (Wilder) wasn't too concerned, even though he was also the producer. He was more concerned about how the man who made it felt when all his work sank to the bottom of the Loch Ness. He went over and comforted him." The original monster prop was located on the bottom of Loch Ness in April 2016 during a survey of the loch by an underwater robot.

By the time of filming, Sir Christopher Lee had become famous as Count Dracula. When he and Billy Wilder walked on the shores of Loch Ness at dusk, with bats circling overhead, Wilder said to him, "You must feel quite at home here."

Goofs

The events start in August 1887 and apparently take place in the following weeks or, at most, months. However, Mycroft Holmes tells Queen Victoria that Kaiser Wilhelm II had Count Zeppelin working on dirigibles that could drop bombs on Buckingham Palace. Wilhelm II did not become Kaiser until 15 June 1888, and Zeppelin did not start constructing rigid airships until the 1890s.

When Holmes and Watson are visiting Mycroft in the Diogenes Club, Holmes mentions the Club's supposed quest to find the Abominable Snowman. The term "Abominable Snowman" wasn't coined until a journalist did so in 1921, many years after our story.

In the grave-digging scene, the lantern appears to have an electric light rather than a flame.

Chisum. As one of the founders of the town of Lincoln, John Chisum is increasingly worried as Lawrence Murphy moves in on the local stores, bank and land by questionable means.

Chisum and fellow honest ranch owner Henry Tunstall try and use the law, but Murphy owns that too. Confrontation threatens and Tunstall's man Billy Bonney is not slow to get involved.

Men wore hats outside in Old West nearly 100% of the time. It was so rare that a man would remove his hat outside for more than brief periods that it would be the subject of discussion when or if it occurred.

Multiple scenes in the film show men outside, hatless, and this is ignored or treated as "normal."

The film cost $4,000,000 to produce and the box office returned $6,000,000.

Trivia

Although clearly labelled as the older man, at 58 Patric Knowles was actually four years younger than John Wayne. Wayne's character, John Chisum, died five or six years after the events portrayed in this movie, at age 60. In real life cattle Baron John Tunstall was 24 when he was murdered; he was played by the 58-year-old Knowles. The real John Chisum was 54 at the time the events in this film occurred, but he was played by the 62-year-old Wayne.

The Chisum Ranch house in this film is the exact house used in Big Jake (1971), a John Wayne western made a year later. Note the scenery around the ranch.

The Zoom in and zoom out sequences of Chisum sitting on his horse on the hillside at the beginning and end of the movie are the same footage. The original shot was the zoom out used at the end. That was reversed to produce the zoom in used at the beginning.

Goofs

Men wore hats outside in Old West nearly 100% of the time. It was so rare that a man would remove his hat outside for more than brief periods that it would be the subject of discussion when or if it occurred. Multiple scenes in the film show men outside, hatless, and this is ignored or treated as "normal."

The clothing worn by the characters in the film was not period correct. This included full front button shorts, hats which were not worn during the 1880s and women's dresses which were far too snug for the period.

Tunstall and Billy Bonney are standing by their horses and talking to Jess Evans who has just ridden in to town. In three consecutive shots of the scene, Tunstall alternately has his pipe in his mouth, after which it is gone, and then re-appears.

MUSIC 1970

The table below is a list of all the number one's in 1970, the name of the single and number of weeks at number one.

Reached number one	Artist(s)	Single	Weeks at number one
January 3, 1970	B. J. Thomas	"Raindrops Keep Fallin' On My Head"	4
January 31, 1970	The Jackson 5	"I Want You Back"	1
February 7, 1970	Shocking Blue	"Venus"	1
February 14, 1970	Sly & the Family Stone	"Everybody Is a Star"	2
February 28, 1970	Simon & Garfunkel	"Bridge Over Troubled Water"	6
April 11, 1970	The Beatles	"Let It Be"	2
April 25, 1970	The Jackson 5	"ABC"	2
May 9, 1970	The Guess Who	"American Woman" / "No Sugar Tonight"	3
May 30, 1970	Ray Stevens	"Everything Is Beautiful"	2
June 13, 1970	The Beatles	"The Long and Winding Road" / "For You Blue"	2
June 27, 1970	The Jackson 5	"The Love You Save"	2
July 11, 1970	Three Dog Night	"Mama Told Me (Not to Come)"	2
July 25, 1970	The Carpenters	"(They Long to Be) Close to You"	4
August 22, 1970	Bread	"Make It with You"	1
August 29, 1970	Edwin Starr	"War"	3
September 19, 1970	Diana Ross	"Ain't No Mountain High Enough"	3
October 10, 1970	Neil Diamond	"Cracklin' Rosie"	1
October 17, 1970	The Jackson 5	"I'll Be There"	5
November 21, 1970	The Partridge Family	"I Think I Love You"	3
December 12, 1970	Smokey Robinson & the Miracles	"The Tears of a Clown"	2
December 26, 1970	George Harrison	"My Sweet Lord" / "Isn't It a Pity"	4

B.J. Thomas

"Raindrops Keep Fallin' On My Head"

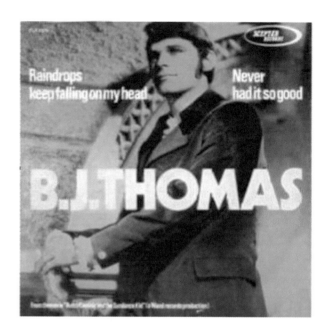

"Raindrops Keep Fallin' on My Head" is a song written by Hal David and Burt Bacharach for the 1969 film Butch Cassidy and the Sundance Kid. It won an Oscar for Best Original Song. David and Bacharach also won Best Original Score. The song was recorded by B. J. Thomas in seven takes, after Bacharach expressed dissatisfaction with the first six. In the film version of the song, Thomas had been recovering from laryngitis, which made his voice sound more abrasive than in the 7-inch release. The film version featured a separate vaudeville-style instrumental break in double time while Paul Newman performed bicycle stunts.

The single by B. J. Thomas reached No. 1 on charts in the United States, Canada, and Norway and reached No. 38 in the UK Singles Chart. It topped the Billboard Hot 100 for four weeks in January 1970 and was also the first American No. 1 hit of the 1970s

The Jackson 5

"I Want You Back"

"I Want You Back" is the first national single by the Jackson 5. It was released by Motown on October 7, 1969, and became the first number-one hit for the band on January 31, 1970. It was performed on the band's first television appearances, on October 18, 1969 on Diana Ross's The Hollywood Palace and on their milestone performance on December 14, 1969 on The Ed Sullivan Show.

The song, along with a B-side remake of "Who's Lovin' You" by Smokey Robinson & the Miracles, was the only single to be released from the Jackson 5's first album, Diana Ross Presents the Jackson 5. It went to number one on the Soul singles chart for four weeks and held the number-one position on the Billboard Hot 100 singles chart for the week ending January 31, 1970. "I Want You Back" was ranked 121st on Rolling Stone's list of The 500 Greatest Songs of All Time.

Shocking Blue

"Venus"

"**Venus**" is a song by Dutch rock band Shocking Blue, released as a single from their second studio album, At Home (1969). Written by Robbie van Leeuwen, the song topped the charts in nine countries. In 1981, it was used to open the "Stars on 45" medley. In 1986, English girl group Bananarama covered "Venus" for their third studio album, True Confessions, reaching number one in six countries. The composition has been featured in numerous films, television shows and commercials, and covered dozens of times by artists around the world. Released in late 1969 as a single from the group's second studio album, At Home "Venus" reached number one on the Billboard Hot 100 on 7 February 1970. On 28 January 1970, it was certified gold by the Recording Industry Association of America (RIAA) for sales in excess of one million copies in the United States.

Sly & the Family Stone

"Everybody Is a Star"

"**Everybody Is a Star**", released in December 1969, is song written by Sylvester Stewart and recorded by Sly and the Family Stone. The song, released as the b-side to the band's 1970 single "Thank You (Falettinme Be Mice Elf Agin)", reached number one on the Billboard Hot 100 in February 1970 at a time when chart position for both sides of the single were measured equally and not independently. "Star" was intended to be included on an in-progress album with "Thank You" and "Hot Fun in the Summertime"; the LP was never completed, and the three tracks were instead included on the band's 1970 Greatest Hits compilation.

The single was the final classic-era Family Stone recording; it would be 23 months until the next release, the single "Family Affair" in late 1971.

Simon and Garfunkel

"Bridge over Troubled Water"

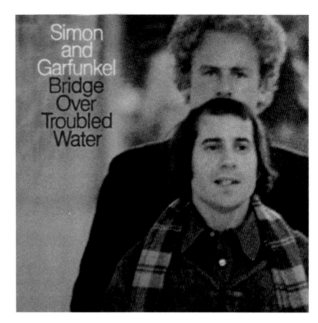

Bridge over Troubled Water was released on January 26, 1970, and several re-releases followed. The album was mixed and released in both stereo and quadraphonic. "Bridge over Troubled Water" is a song by American music duo Simon & Garfunkel. Produced by the duo and Roy Halee, the song was released as the follow-up single to "The Boxer" in January 1970. The song is featured on their fifth studio album, Bridge over Troubled Water (1970). Composed by singer-songwriter Paul Simon, the song is performed on piano and carries the influence of gospel music. The original studio recording employs elements of Phil Spector's "Wall of Sound" technique using L.A. session musicians from the Wrecking Crew. Bridge Over Troubled Water made number 1 in the UK in March 1970 and stayed there for 3 weeks.

The Beatles

"Let It Be"

"Let It Be" is a song by the English rock band the Beatles, released on 6 March 1970 as a single, and (in an alternate mix) as the title track of their album Let It Be. It was written and sung by Paul McCartney. The single version of the song, produced by George Martin, features a softer guitar solo and the orchestral section mixed low, while the album version, produced by Phil Spector, features a more aggressive guitar solo and the orchestral sections mixed up.

At the time, it had the highest debut on the Billboard Hot 100, beginning its chart run at number 6. It was their final single before McCartney announced his departure from the band. Both the Let It Be album and the US single "The Long and Winding Road" were released after McCartney's announced departure from and the subsequent break-up of the group.

Jackson 5

"ABC"

"**ABC**" is a 1970 #1 hit by The Jackson 5. It was released on February 24. "ABC" knocked The Beatles' "Let It Be" off the top of the Billboard Hot 100 in 1970, and was #1 on the soul singles chart for four weeks.

Written with a similar structure and feel as the Jacksons' first hit of 1970, "I Want You Back". ABC was performed on television on American Bandstand (February 21, 1970), The Ed Sullivan Show (May 10, 1970), and The Flip Wilson Show (November 4, 1971), among many other broadcasts. "ABC" is considered one of the band's signature songs. It is one of the shortest titles to hit #1, and is the first alphabetically in a list of #1 hits on the Billboard Hot 100. The upbeat lyrics compare learning to love to learning the alphabet. This makes it similar to Len Barry's 1965 hit "1-2-3." The song is considered by some to be one of the first disco songs.

Mungo Jerry

"No Sugar Tonight/New Mother Nature"

"**No Sugar Tonight/New Mother Nature**" is a song by the Canadian rock band The Guess Who. It was released on their 1970 album American Woman, and was released on the B-side of the "American Woman" single without the "New Mother Nature" section. The single was officially released as "American Woman/No Sugar Tonight" and peaked at #1 on the RPM magazine charts (three weeks) and #1 on the Billboard Hot 100. In Cash Box, which at the time ranked sides independently, "No Sugar Tonight" reached #39.

The song was covered by The Shirelles on their Happy and in Love album released in 1971, and by Bang on their Mother/Bow to the King album (Capitol Records, SMAS-11110) released in 1972. Capitol subsequently released the song as a single but it failed to chart. Widespread Panic included covers of the song on their live albums Live at The Classic Center and Live at The Tabernacle.

Ray Stevens

"Everything Is Beautiful"

"**Everything Is Beautiful**" is a song written, composed, and performed by Ray Stevens. It has appeared on many of Stevens' albums, including one named after the song, and has become a pop standard and common in religious performances. The children heard singing the chorus of the song, using the hymn, "Jesus Loves the Little Children", are from the Oak Hill Elementary School in Nashville, Tennessee. This group includes Stevens' two daughters. The song was responsible for two wins at the Grammy Awards of 1971: Grammy Award for Best Male Pop Vocal Performance for Ray Stevens and Grammy Award for Best Inspirational Performance for Jake Hess. Stevens' recording was the Number 1 song on the Billboard Hot 100 for two weeks in the summer of 1970. The song also spent three weeks atop the adult contemporary chart. Many country stations played the song, with it peaking at number 39 on Billboard's chart.

Smokey Robinson and The Miracles

"The Long and Winding Road"

"**The Long and Winding Road**" is a song by the English rock band the Beatles from their 1970 album Let It Be. It was written by Paul McCartney and credited to Lennon–McCartney. When issued as a single in May 1970, a month after the Beatles' break-up, it became the group's 20th and last number-one hit on the Billboard Hot 100 chart in the United States. It was the final single released by the quartet. The main recording of the song took place in January 1969 and featured a sparse musical arrangement. When preparing the tapes from these sessions for release in April 1970, producer Phil Spector added orchestral and choral overdubs. Spector's modifications angered McCartney to the point that when the latter made his case in the British High Court for the Beatles' disbandment, he cited the treatment of "The Long and Winding Road" as one of six reasons for doing so.

Jackson 5

"The Love You Save"

"The Love You Save" is a 1970 number-one hit single recorded by The Jackson 5 for Motown Records. It held the number-one spot on the soul singles chart for six weeks and the number-one position on the Billboard Hot 100 singles chart for two weeks, from June 27 to July 4, 1970 (in the UK Top 40 chart, it peaked at number 7 in August 1970). The song is the third of the four-in-a-row Jackson 5 number-ones released (the others were "I Want You Back", "ABC", and "I'll Be There"). Billboard ranked the record as the No. 16 song of 1970, one slot behind the Jackson 5's "ABC".

"The Love You Save" features side vocals of Jermaine Jackson singing alongside Michael in the final "Stop! The love you save may be your own", beside Marlon, Tito and Jackie.

Three Dog Night

"Mama Told Me Not to Come"

"Mama Told Me Not to Come" also written as "Mama Told Me (Not to Come)", is a song by American singer-songwriter Randy Newman written for Eric Burdon's first solo album in 1966. Three Dog Night's 1970 cover topped the US pop singles chart. Tom Jones and the Stereophonics' version also hit No. 4 on the UK Singles Chart in 2000.

Three Dog Night released a longer, rock 'n roll and funk-inspired version (titled "Mama Told Me (Not to Come)") on It Ain't Easy.

Three Dog Night's had the same 3/4 by 2/4 time change as Eric Burdon's version and featured Cory Wells singing lead in an almost humorous vocal style, Jimmy Greenspoon playing a Wurlitzer electric piano, and Michael Allsup playing guitar.

The Carpenters

"(They Long to Be) Close to You"

"(They Long to Be) Close to You" is a song recorded by American duo the Carpenters for their second studio album Close to You (1970). It was written by Burt Bacharach and Hal David, and produced by Jack Daugherty. Released on May 15, 1970, the song topped both the US Billboard Hot 100 and Adult Contemporary charts. It also reached the top of the Canadian and Australian charts, and peaked at number six on the charts of both the UK and Ireland.

"(They Long to Be) Close to You" earned the Carpenters a Grammy Award for Best Contemporary Performance by a Duo, Group or Chorus in 1971. It became the first of three Grammy Awards they would win during their careers. The song was certified Gold by the Recording Industry Association of America (RIAA) on August 12, 1970.

Bread

"Make It with You"

"Make It with You" is a song written by David Gates and originally recorded by the pop-rock group Bread, of which Gates was a member. Only Gates and drummer Mike Botts appear on the song which was a #1 hit.

The song first appeared on Bread's 1970 album, On the Waters. Released as a single that June, it was the group's first top-ten hit on the Billboard Hot 100 singles chart and spent the week of August 22, 1970, at number one, their only single to do so; it also reached #5 on the UK Singles Chart.

Billboard ranked "Make It with You" as the No. 13 song of 1970, and it was certified gold by the RIAA for sales of over one million copies.

Edwin Starr

"War"

"War" is a counterculture-era soul song written by Norman Whitfield and Barrett Strong for the Motown label in 1969.

Whitfield first produced the song – an obvious anti-Vietnam War protest – with The Temptations as the original vocalists. After Motown began receiving repeated requests to release "War" as a single, Whitfield re-recorded the song with Edwin Starr as the vocalist, with the label deciding to withhold the Temptations' version from single release so as not to alienate their more conservative fans. Starr's version of "War" was a No. 1 hit on the Billboard Hot 100 chart in 1970, and is not only the most successful and well-known record of his career, but it is also one of the most popular protest songs ever recorded. It was one of 161 songs on the Clear Channel no-play list after September 11, 2001

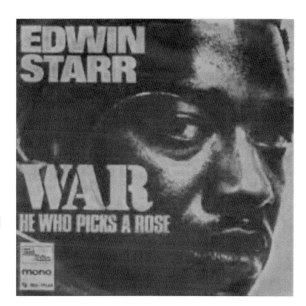

Diana Ross

"Ain't No Mountain High Enough"

"Ain't No Mountain High Enough" In spring 1970, after the Top 20 success of her first solo single, "Reach Out and Touch (Somebody's Hand)", Ashford and Simpson had Ross re-record "Ain't No Mountain High Enough". Initially, Ross was apprehensive, but was convinced to make the recording. The remake was similar to gospel with elements of classical music strings (provided by the Detroit Symphony Orchestra), spoken word passages from Ross, with The Andantes, Jimmy Beavers, Jo Armstead, Ashford & Simpson and Brenda Evans and Billie Calvin of The Undisputed Truth as backing singers, giving the song a soul and gospel vocal element.

In 2017, "Ain't No Mountain High Enough" was remixed by Eric Kupper, StoneBridge and Chris Cox, amongst others, on Motown/UMe. The new remix went to number one on the Billboard Dance Club Songs chart.

Neil Diamond

"Cracklin' Rosie"

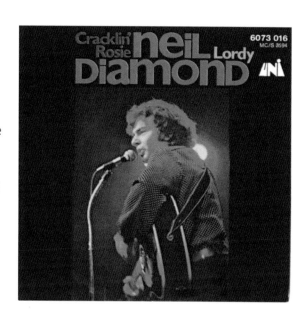

"Cracklin' Rosie" is a song written and recorded by Neil Diamond in 1970, with instrumental backing by L.A. session musicians from the Wrecking Crew, including Hal Blaine on drums, Larry Knechtel on keyboards, Joe Osborn on bass, Al Casey on guitar and Gene Estes on percussion - arranged by Don Randi, and was included on his album Tap Root Manuscript. In October 1970; the song became Diamond's first American #1 hit on The Billboard Hot 100, and his third to sell a million copies.

It was his breakthrough single on the UK Singles Chart, reaching #3 for four weeks in November and December. Billboard ranked the record as the No. 17 song of 1970. It also reached #2 on both the Australian Singles Chart and the Irish Singles Chart. Its best performance was in New Zealand, where it stayed at number one for 5 weeks at the end of the year.

Jackson 5

"I'll Be There"

"I'll Be There" is the first single released on the Third Album by The Jackson 5. It's written by Berry Gordy, Hal Davis, Bob West, and Willie Hutch.

The song was recorded by The Jackson 5 and released by Motown Records on August 28, 1970 as the first single from their Third Album on the same date. Produced by the songwriters, "I'll Be There" was The Jackson 5's fourth number-one hit in a row (after "I Want You Back" in 1969, "ABC" and "The Love You Save" earlier in 1970), making them the first black male group to achieve four consecutive number-one pop hits.

"I'll Be There" is also notable as the most successful single released by Motown during its "Detroit era" (1959–72).

The Partridge Family

"I Think I Love You"

"**I Think I Love You**" is a song composed by songwriter Tony Romeo in 1970. It was released as the debut single by The Partridge Family pop group, featuring David Cassidy on lead vocals and Shirley Jones on background vocals. The Partridge Family version was a number-one hit on the Billboard Hot 100 in November 1970. The alternative rock band Voice of the Beehive scored a hit version of their own in 1991. There have also been many other versions of this song from artists such as Perry Como, Kaci Battaglia and Katie Cassidy. The single was produced by Wes Farrell and issued on Bell Records a month before the debut of the network television musical sitcom The Partridge Family. During the show's first season the song was featured on the show twice as it was climbing the actual Billboard chart. The single hit number one on the U.S. Billboard Hot 100 chart and in Canada

Smokey Robinson

"The Tears of a Clown"

"**The Tears of a Clown**" is a song written by Hank Cosby, Smokey Robinson, and Stevie Wonder and originally recorded by Smokey Robinson & the Miracles for the Tamla Records label subsidiary of Motown, first appearing on the 1967 album Make It Happen. It was re-released in the United Kingdom as a single in July 1970, and it became a #1 hit on the UK Singles Chart for the week ending 12 September 1970. Subsequently, Motown released "The Tears of a Clown" as a single in the United States as well, where it quickly became a #1 hit on both the Billboard Hot 100 and R&B Singles charts.

This song is an international multi-million seller and a 2002 Grammy Hall of Fame inductee. Its success led Miracles lead singer, songwriter, and producer Smokey Robinson, who had announced plans to leave the act, to stay until 1972.

George Harrison

"My Sweet Lord" / "Isn't It a Pity"

"My Sweet Lord" is a song by English musician George Harrison, released in November 1970 on his triple album All Things Must Pass. It was also released as a single, Harrison's first as a solo artist, and topped charts worldwide; it was the biggest-selling single of 1971 in the UK. In America and Britain, the song was the first number-one single by an ex-Beatle. Harrison originally gave the song to his fellow Apple Records artist Billy Preston to record; this version, which Harrison co-produced, appeared on Preston's Encouraging Words album in September 1970.

Later in the 1970s, "My Sweet Lord" was at the centre of a heavily publicised copyright infringement suit due to its similarity to the Ronnie Mack song "He's So Fine", a 1963 hit for the New York girl group the Chiffons.

WORLD EVENTS

January

1 Unix time became the standard for timestamps in computer programming at 00:00:00 UTC as the new year was ushered in at Greenwich, England. "Unix simply counts seconds since New Year's Day 1970," in comparing the difference between two different times, a programmer noted in 2005, adding "An advantage to storing time in this fashion is that there was no inherent Y2K problem with Unix-based systems... The disadvantage is that the Y2K problem has simply been postponed," since the number of seconds in the "Unix epoch" are stored on a 32-bit integer system "and sometime in the year 2038, the number of seconds since the beginning of the Unix epoch will be larger than a 32-bit integer." Unix time at the beginning of January 1, 2020 UTC will be 1577851200.

3 The final recording of a song by The Beatles took place at the Abbey Road Studios in London for inclusion on the group's last released album, Let It Be, as Paul McCartney, George Harrison and Ringo Starr completed a song written by Harrison, "I Me Mine".

4 Keith Moon, drummer for the classic rock band The Who, ran over and killed his bodyguard and chauffeur, Neil Boland, after getting intoxicated and fleeing from a hostile crowd of English youths in Hatfield, Hertfordshire. Boland had driven Moon's Bentley automobile to Hatfield so that Moon, his wife and two friends could attend the opening of the Red Lion discothèque, and Boland had gotten out to the car to keep the crowd away. The death of Boland, who was dragged underneath the Bentley while Moon was trying to drive away from the scene, was ruled to be an accident by investigators, and Moon, who would die of a drug overdose in 1978, was never charged with a crime.

January

5 A 7.1 magnitude earthquake struck China's Yunnan province less than a minute after 1:00 in the morning local time (1700 UTC on 4 January). The Chinese government did not acknowledge the disaster until four days later, when Radio Peking reported that the local populace was acting "in the revolutionary spirit, fearing neither hardship nor death" and that "the people creatively applied the thoughts of Mao Tse-tung and fought the natural disaster all in one hart and with 100-fold confidence." According to statistics later released by the People's Republic of China, the quake killed 14,621 people in Kunming and surrounding Tonghai County, and injured 26,783.

7 The Kaizer Chiefs F.C. professional soccer football club was founded in the Soweto township of Johannesburg, South Africa. Kaizer Motaung, a black soccer football star who had become well known in the United States with the Atlanta Chiefs pro soccer team, created the Kaizer Chiefs to compete with another Soweto team, the Orlando Pirates. The two clubs would become founding members of the National Professional Soccer League in 1971, and then would be part of the merger between the all-nonwhite NPSL and South Africa's all-white pro soccer circuit, the National Football League, in 1977.

12 In one of Australia's most famous mysteries, Cheryl Grimmer, a three-year-old girl, was kidnapped from a beach in Wollongong, New South Wales. A suspect would be arrested 47 years later, based on a confession that he had made in a police interview after the crime, but the charges were dropped after a judge ruled that the confession could not be admitted into evidence at the trial.

13 Fifty-eight people were killed in two separate airline crashes on the same day. A Faucett Airlines DC-4 disappeared in Peru while en route from Trujillo to Juanjui Earlier, a DC-3, described as the only aircraft owned by Polynesian Airlines, crashed on takeoff from Apia Faleolo airport, killing all 27 passengers and three crew in its attempt to fly to Pago Pago.

15 Will Owen, a British Member of Parliament who had represented Morpeth in the House of Commons since 1954, was arrested on charges of espionage and ordered held in gaol without bond. In addition to his parliamentary duties, Owen was the chairman of a Mayfair travel agency, Berolina that specialized in tourism in East Germany. Jock Wilson, the Commander of Scotland Yard, personally placed Owen under arrest on charges of communicating information "useful to an enemy" between 1961 and 1969.

18 The Tomb of Karl Marx was vandalized by explosives placed by unknown perpetrators at Highgate Cemetery in London. Although Marx, a German economist whose theories became the basis for the planned economies used in Communist nations, had died in 1893, the 12-foot high memorial had more recently been created in 1956. More than 45 years later, a London newspaper, the Camden New Journal, would report that the vandals' apparent plan had been to saw an opening in the face of the memorial (a bust of Marx's head) and to fill the hollow shell with explosives. Although the nose was partially sawed through, the participants went to a second plan and set off the bomb in front of the monument instead.

20 Samsung Electronics, now the world's largest manufacturer of consumer electronics, was incorporated in South Korea as Samsung Electric Industries. The company was created as a new division of the Samsung Group, which had been founded in 1938 as a wholesaler of groceries.

21 The government of Iraq suppressed an attempted coup against President Ahmed Hassan al-Bakr that had started the night before, then arrested, convicted an executed 22 people in the afternoon. Radio Baghdad announced the foiling of the plot at noon. Over the next several hours, a special three-man court meted out the sentences for those found guilty.

January

24 | At Cardiff, the Wales national rugby union team and the South Africa's national team, the Springboks, played to a 6-6 draw, bringing an end to the 1969–70 South Africa rugby union tour of Britain and Ireland and marking the first time that Wales did not lose to South Africa in international competition. In the final seconds of the match, Gareth Edwards downed the ball across the goal line to score a try (at the time worth 3 points rather than 5) "as if his life depended on it... to the delirious and relieved roar of the Welsh crowd, who could hardly believe their good fortune." Edwards's two-point conversion kick failed, sparing the Springboks from an 8-6 loss.

30 | The People's Republic of China made its first successful test of an intercontinental ballistic missile (ICBM). The DF-4 (Dong Feng or "east wind") had a range of 4,500 kilometers (2,800 mi) and was China's first two-stage missile and could carry a one megaton nuclear warhead.

February

1 | At least 236 people were killed, and 360 injured in Argentina's worst railroad disaster. The high speed luxury train "La Mixta" was 25 miles (40 km) north of Buenos Aires at the end of a 925 miles (1,489 km) trip from Tucuman, and carried about 400 passengers in 21 rail cars. Ahead, a commuter train that was crowded with 1,000 passengers in 10 crowded cars, had stalled on the same tracks, but there was no signal to warn the luxury train, which was moving at 65 miles per hour (105 km/h) before impact. Most of the casualties of the wreck were on the commuter train.

6 | Aeroflot Flight U-45 crashed in the Soviet Union's Uzbek SSR (now Uzbekistan) during its approach to Samarkand after a 162 miles (261 km) flight that had originated in Tashkent. Only 14 of the 98 people on board survived. A misreading of the radar data by an air traffic controller in Samarkand led to prematurely clearing the Ilyushin Il-18 airliner for descent, and the plane impacted on a mountain slope on the Zarafshan Range at an altitude of 1,500 meters (4,900 ft). Consistent with Soviet policy at the time, the accident was not mentioned in the media.

8 | Four days after running aground on Cerberus Rock within Chedabucto Bay off of Nova Scotia, the oil tanker SS Arrow broke apart and began spilling its cargo of petroleum into the Nova Scotian waters. The discharge of 10,000 tons (9,800 long tons; 11,000 short tons) of oil (over 11 million liters or 3 million U.S. gallons) and befouled 300 kilometers (190 mi) of coastline. It remains the worst oil spill in Canadian history (the 1988 by the sinking of the supertanker Odyssey was 1,300 kilometers (810 mi) from Nova Scotia and drifted away from Canada).

10 | An avalanche of snow killed at least 39 young skiers as it smashed into the bottom floors of a chalet at the Alpine resort of Val-d'Isère in France. At 8:05 in the morning, as residents were having breakfast, more than 100,000 cubic yards of snow and debris swept down the crest of the Le Dome mountain of the Vanoise massif range. Residents had only seconds to get out after a tremendous roar heralded the approach of the debris.

13 | The first heavy metal album, Black Sabbath went on sale in Britain. Black Sabbath had been formed in the English city of Birmingham in 1968 by guitarist and chief songwriter Tony Iommi, lead singer Ozzy Osbourne, drummer Bill Ward, and bassistGeezer Butler. Within weeks, the debut record would be the eighth bestselling rock album on the British charts, and would be released in the United States on June 1.

14 | The British rock band The Who performed a concert at the 2,100 seat University of Leeds Refectory in England. Recorded at the concert, the record album Live at Leeds was described by Nik Cohn of The New York Times as "the best live rock album ever made" and by another critic as "one of the gold standards in live rock & roll".

21 | All 47 people aboard Swissair Flight 330 were killed when the Convair 990 jet was damaged in midflight by a terrorist bomb. The flight departed Zurich at 1:14 in the afternoon, bound for Tel Aviv and, seven minutes later, the bomb's barometric pressure mechanism triggered the explosion in the cargo hold when the Convair reached an altitude 4,300 meters (14,100 ft). The pilot, Karl Berlinger, turned the plane back toward Zurich upon detecting the loss in cabin pressure, and the crew realized there was fire at 1:26 before smoke filled the cabin. By 1:33, the plane was so full of smoke that the crew couldn't see the instruments and Berlinger radioed his last message to the tower (in English) — "We are crashing. Goodbye everybody." The jet crashed in the Unterwald forest, at Würenlingen, went into a dive, and impacted at a speed of 770 kilometers per hour (480 mph), obliterating the plane and everyone and everything onboard.

22 | Keith Sapsford, a 14 year old boy from Australia, fell to his death from an airliner after trying to stowaway inside the wheel well of the DC-8 jet. Sapsford had climbed in and was lying on top of a door to the wheel compartment, which opened at an altitude of 200 feet (61 m) when the wheels of the Japan Air Lines jet were retracting. The incident was witnessed by 350 people watching from an observation deck at the Sydney International Airport, and was photographed by one of the bystanders who was testing a new camera; the picture would be reprinted in newspapers around the world.

25 | A routine in an episode of the children's TV series Sesame Street was performed for the first time and would soon become a best-selling record, as the Muppet character Ernie sang "Rubber Duckie" (with Jim Henson supplying the voice) as an ode to the rubber duck bathtub toy. The latex toy duck had been invented by sculptor Peter Ganine, who applied for a patent on December 29, 1947 and received U.S. Patent No. 153,514 on April 26, 1949. The song itself was written by Jeff Moss and arranged by Joe Raposo.

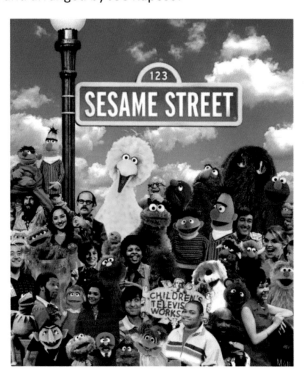

2 | Rhodesia severed its last tie with the United Kingdom and declared it a republic, with former British solicitor Clifford DuPont signing the proclamation dissolving the parliament and becoming the first President of Rhodesia. DuPont had been the administrator of Rhodesia since 1965, when Prime Minister Ian Smith, who continued as the head of government, had declared the African colony's independence from the United Kingdom. The republic's new constitution continued the policy of white minority rule. Rhodesia's 341,000 white citizens, representing seven percent of the population, maintained authority over the nation's 4,500,000 nonwhite residents.

4 | All 57 of the crew of France's Marine Nationale submarine Eurydice were killed after the vessel made a practice dive and never resurfaced. The Daphné-class submarine was in 2,000 feet (610 m) deep waters in the Mediterranean Sea off of Cape Camarat, after sailing from its base at Saint-Tropez. At 7:00 a.m. local time, it radioed that it was making a dive and less than an hour later, signs of a violent explosion were detected. An oil slick and debris from the Eurydice were found late in the afternoon by rescue ships.

8 | A team of assassins in Nicosia attempted to assassinate Makarios III, the President of Cyprus, riddling the presidential helicopter with machine gun fire as it was lifting off from the rooftop of his residence, Nicosia Palace. Palace guards fired at the assassins, Greek Cypriot members of the EOKA group advocating the island's annexation by Greece, who had taken a position on the roof of a nearby building. President Makarios escaped injury; the helicopter pilot was critically wounded by three bullets, but managed to safely land the copter .

10 | France made its first successful launch of its new 78 feet (24 m) tall, three-stage Diamant-B rocket, and the first satellite launch from its new Guiana Space Centre. Prior to building the rocket base in Kourou in the South American colony of French Guiana, the French space program had launched four satellites from Hammaguir in the Republic of Algeria. The payload was two West German satellites, Wika and Mika, sent into orbit to study the Van Allen radiation belt; vibrations from the first rocket stage, however, disabled the Mika communication system.

12 | For the first time in British history, citizens younger than 21 were able to cast ballots in a parliamentary election. The opportunity came in the by-election, to fill a vacancy in the Bridgwater constituency in the House of Commons that followed the October 31 death of Gerald Wills. Miss Trudy Sellick, a secretary who had turned 18 years old earlier in the day, registered the first under-21 vote in British history; she was in line when the polling station at North Newton, Somerset, opened at 7:00 in the morning. Conservative Party candidate Tom King began a 31 year career as a Member of Parliament, winning the by-election with 55 percent of the votes cast.

13 | The sinking of the Iranian ship Viaqtar killed 105 of the 180 people on board. The ship, bringing Muslims back to Iran after their pilgrimage to Mecca, capsized and sank off of the coast of Abu Dhabi.

16 | The New English Bible, an updated translation, went on sale worldwide after the completion of translation of the Old Testament. Rather than making a revision of previous English versions, a team of Biblical scholars worked from Hebrew language texts, and the publishers of the universities at Oxford and Cambridge stated that the new version was "as truthful as human skill could make it— and carried out by the best scholars and translators that the churches possessed". The release came a little more than nine years after the release of the NEB New Testament translation on March 14, 1961.

26 | North Vietnam refused an offer by South Vietnam for the release and repatriation of 343 wounded or ill prisoners of war, declaring that there were no members of the North Vietnamese Army in the south. The Hanoi representatives at the Paris Peace Talks asserted that the captives were, instead, "illegally arrested patriots" from among South Vietnamese citizens rebelling against the Saigon government.

27 | In the largest air battle in the Middle East since the end of the 1967 Six-Day War, approximately 80 jets fought in the skies over the Port Suez, with 40 Egyptian MiG fighters and 40 Israeli Air Force Phantom jets. The Israeli fighters returned home safely, and reported shooting down five of the Egyptian MiGs.

28 | A 7.2 magnitude earthquake struck western Turkey at 11:02 p.m. local time (21:02 UTC) and killed 1,086 people, most of them in the town of Gediz. The town, which had been damaged by earthquakes in the past, would later be relocated to safer ground 7 kilometers (4.3 mi) southwest of its prior location.

29 | Eleven days after the overthrow of Prince Sihanouk, North Vietnamese Army forces invaded eastern Cambodia to assist the Cambodian Communist Khmer Rouge. The NVA would come within 15 miles (24 km) of taking the capital, Phnom Penh, before being pushed back in a counteroffensive.

31 | Japan Airlines Flight 351 was hijacked by the Japanese Red Army terrorist group, along with its 131 passengers and crew of seven, shortly after its takeoff from Tokyo on a flight to Fukuoka, and ordered to fly to North Korea. The Army group released 22 of the passengers at Fukuoka, then demanded to be flown to North Korea with 100 others. South Korean authorities tricked the hijackers by permitting the Boeing 727 to land at the airfield in Kimpo, on the South Korean side of the Han River, and then sending out soldiers dressed in North Korean Army uniforms and placing propaganda signs at the airfield to give the illusion that the plane was at the North Korean capital of Pyongyang, a ploy that failed. The Red Army freed the rest of its captives on April 3 after Japan's Vice Minister of Transport volunteered to take their place, and flew onward to North Korea.

3 | In South Korea, the Japanese Red Army terrorist group accepted a proposal that Japan's Vice Minister for Transport, Shinjiro Yamamura, take the place of the remaining 100 passengers held captive on Japan Airlines Flight 351. The Boeing 727 jet had been hijacked 79 hours earlier while en route from Tokyo to Fukuoka, and the crew had landed at the Kimpo airfield outside of Seoul rather than acceding to the nine hijackers' demand that they be flown to North Korea. The jet then flew onward to the Pyongyang airport in North Korea with Yamamura and the crew of three. Yamamura and flight crew Shinji Isida, Teiichi Esaki and Toshio Aihara were allowed to fly the Boeing 727 from Pyongyang back to Tokyo the next day.

4 | The disposal of the remains of Adolf Hitler was carried out at the Soviet Union's military base in Magdeburg, East Germany. Only the commander of the base was aware that the burnt skeletons of Hitler, Eva Braun, General Hans Krebs, Joseph Goebbels, Magda Goebbels and the Goebbels children, had been interred there. Hitler's skull had been sent to Moscow in 1945, where they were placed in the State Archives in Moscow. In that the base was scheduled to be relinquished to East Germany, the commander consulted KGB Director Yuri Andropov for instructions. To prevent the site from becoming a shrine for neo-Nazis, Andropov ordered that the grave's contents be crushed, burned and scattered. The process was completed the next day at Schönebeck, and what was left over was dumped into the Elbe River.

6 | King Frederik IX of Denmark overturned his Bentley convertible automobile while driving on a Copenhagen street, but was not seriously injured. After climbing out of his car, which skidded on a slippery street.. hit the curb and landed on its side", the King rode part of the way back to the Amalienberg Palace in an ambulance, then asked the driver to stop, got out, and walked the rest of the way, "apparently wary that his arrival by ambulance might cause alarm."

10 | With the page one headline "PAUL QUITS THE BEATLES", Britain's national daily tabloid newspaper, the Daily Mirror, broke the story that Paul McCartney was leaving The Beatles. McCartney's parting of ways with John Lennon, and bandmates George Harrison and Ringo Starr, effectively brought a permanent end to the most popular rock musician group in history. McCartney issued a press release later in the day in conjunction with promotional copies of his first album as a solo artist, McCartney.

12 | Fifty-two of the surviving 125 crewmen on the Soviet submarine K-8 died when the vessel was flooded with carbon monoxide as they were attempting to extinguish a fire. Four days earlier, eight other crews had been killed when they were sealed off inside sections of the sub during an effort to fight the blaze. The remaining crew had evacuated the sub, but then were ordered to go back inside while it was being towed. After the 20 of the 24 nuclear weapons on board were removed, K-8 sank in the Bay of Biscay, 490 kilometers (300 mi) northwest of Spain, with 60 members of the Soviet Navy and four nuclear torpedoes, in waters 15,350 feet (4,680 m) deep.

16 | At 1:10 in the morning local time, an avalanche buried a tuberculosis sanatorium in the French Alps near Sallanches, killing 74 people. The avalanche, 600 feet (180 m) wide, swept down the Plateau d'Assy and struck the children's wing of the hospital and two nursing dormitories, with 60 feet (18 m) wide wall of snow. Most of the dead were boys under the age of 15, who were asleep when the disaster struck.

19 | The first Lada compact car, the initial offering of the Soviet Union's AvtoVAZ automobile company, rolled off the assembly line of the Volga Automotive Plant in the city of Tolyatti, in the Russian SFSR. The original model, the VAZ-2101, was marketed in Eastern Europe as the "Zhiguli", and in the rest of the world as the "Lada 2101"

23 | The tiny European co-principality of Andorra granted women the right to vote. The decree provided the franchise to 1,300 women in the nation, located in the Pyrenees on the border between Spain and France. It was signed by its joint heads of state, Spain's Bishop of Urgell (Joan Martí i Alanis) and by Martí's fellow co-prince, France's President Georges Pompidou. Women were still ineligible, however, to run for office.

24 | The People's Republic of China became the sixth nation to launch a satellite into Earth orbit, as the spacecraft Dong Fang Hong 1 was sent up using the Changzheng-1 (CZ-1) rocket (named for the Long March). The 346 pounds (157 kg) spacecraft, named for China's national anthem "The East Is Red", transmitted the song continuously as it made an orbit of the Earth every 114 minutes.

27 | An unidentified 58-year-old woman became the first person to receive a heart pacemaker to be powered by an atomic battery, in a four-hour operation at the Hôpital Broussais in Paris. The battery, powered by 150 micrograms of plutonium, reportedly had a life span of 10 years

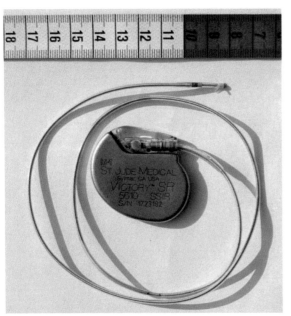 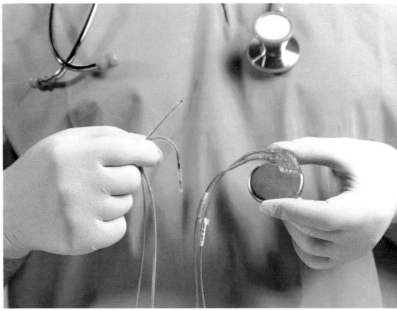

28 | The Roman Catholic Church restrictions on interfaith marriage were partially lifted, as the U.S. National Conference of Catholic Bishops announced a decision made by Pope Paul VI. Previously, under the 1907 papal decree Ne Temere, the non-Catholic husband or wife had to promise to raise any children in the Catholic faith. The new rules eliminated the promise, but did require that the Roman Catholic partner had to promise to do everything in their power "to have all the children baptized and brought up in the Catholic Church" as a prerequisite for the marriage to be recognized by the Church, and for the non-Catholic partner to state understanding of the Catholic obligation. The new rules were to take effect on October 1.

29 | In extra time, the Blues of Chelsea F.C. won England's FA Cup in a replay of the final, after having tied Leeds United, 2 to 2, in the 86th minute of the April 11 game. The replay, watched by a record television audience and played at Old Trafford stadium in Manchester, saw Leeds U. take a 1-0 lead in the first half, until Chelsea's Peter Osgood tied the score in the 78th minute for a 1-1 score at the end of regular play. In the 30 minute extra time period, David Webb headed the ball in at the 104th minute, after a long throw from Ian Hutchinson (whom a reporter said "can throw a ball farther than some men can kick it").

May

6 | The first wristwatch to use an LED display, the Pulsar watch, was introduced by the Hamilton Watch Company with a demonstration on The Tonight Show. After being told that the Pulsar's retail price was $1,500 (equivalent to $9,970 in 2019), Johnny Carson quipped, "The watch will tell you the exact moment you went bankrupt!"

9 | A transit of Mercury (the planet Mercury passing directly between the Sun and the Earth) took place. The Sun-Mercury-Earth alignment happens 13 times in a century and had last taken place on November 7, 1960; it would happen again on November 10, 1973.

12 | The International Olympic Committee chose Montreal as the site for the 1976 Summer Olympics, after it appeared that Moscow would receive the bid. On the first ballot, no bidder got the required 35 vote majority, but Moscow had 28, Montreal 24 and Los Angeles 17, and the Soviet news agency TASS issued an erroneous bulletin celebrating Moscow as the victor. After the IOC narrowed the candidates to two, Montreal received 41 votes and Moscow 28. The 1976 Winter Olympics were awarded to Denver, with the American city finishing ahead of Canada's Vancouver; Sion, Switzerland; and Tampere in Finland. Denver voters would reject funding for the games in a 1972 referendum, and the games would be held instead in the Austrian city of Innsbruck.

18 | At the request of Prime Minister Harold Wilson, Queen Elizabeth II ordered the dissolution of the Parliament of the United Kingdom and set the date for elections for a new House of Commons for Thursday, June 18.

19 | The "Bikini alert state" system was first used for use within the United Kingdom's Ministry of Defense to indicate the level of a threat to UK national security. The system is analogous to the DEFCON indication of defense readiness condition used by the United States Department of Defense, but uses five colors rather than numbers.

23 | The 120-year old Britannia Bridge, a historic landmark that connected the Welsh island of Anglesey to the British mainland, was heavily damaged and rendered impassable by when two teenagers accidentally set it afire. The tubular bridge across the Menai Strait had been built by structural engineer Robert Stephenson and had carried rail traffic since 1850. Although the island's 57,000 residents could still drive across the strait on the Menai Suspension Bridge, the primary source of Anglesey's economy—the use of the port of Holyhead to transport cargoes between the United Kingdom and Ireland—was shut down by the loss of the railroad. A reconstructed bridge would finally open to rail traffic on January 30, 1972, after British Rail's spending of £3,250,000, equivalent to GBP £49,858,000 or US$61,000,000 in 2019.

25	Two days before its conclusion, the 1970 London to Mexico World Cup Rally auto race suffered a fatality when driver Henri "Ido" Marang, was killed, and his co-driver Paul Coltelloni was seriously injured. Marang and Coltelloni had completed about 14,000 miles (23,000 km) of a 16,000 miles (26,000 km) journey and were in last place among 26 vehicles. Marang was driving his Citroën at high speed near Penonomé in Panama when a businessman pulled his car out in front of them.
26	In the Soviet Union, the Tupolev Tu-144 became the first airplane designed for passenger transport to exceed Mach 2. At an altitude of more than 10 miles (16 km), where the speed of sound is less than the 767 miles per hour (1,234 km/h) at sea level, the Tupolev Tu-144 reached a speed of 1,336.5 miles per hour (2,150.9 km/h). "No passenger plane in the world has ever flown at such a speed," the Soviet news agency TASS wrote in its press release about the supersonic jet, flown by test pilot Eduard Yelyan

27	Two British mountain climbers, Don Whillans and Dougal Haston, became the first people to scale the south face of Annapurna I, reaching top of the 26,504 feet (8,078 m) peak as part of an 11-man British expedition team. The first persons to reach Annapurna-1, Maurice Herzog and Luis Lachhenal of France, had ascended by way of the less difficult north face route in 1950.
29	A former President of Argentina, Pedro Arambaru, was kidnapped from his Buenos Aires apartment by two men wearing military uniforms. Aramburu, who had been president from 1955 to 1958, was normally guarded by police, but voluntarily left with the men on the pretext that he was asked to travel with them to Argentina's army command headquarters "for security reasons". The kidnappers, who were members of the Montoneros anti-government group, murdered the former president three days later.
31	Opening ceremonies were held to begin the 1970 FIFA World Cup in Mexico. The opener was a 0-0 tie between the host nation and its Group 1 rival, the team of the Soviet Union. Sixteen teams qualified and played over the next three weeks, with the final held on June 21.

2 | Discovery of Western Europe's first large oil field, located offshore beneath Norway's section of the North Sea was announced by the Phillips Petroleum Company of the U.S., one of four companies in a consortium that had been drilling undersea ". The other partners in the venture were AGIP of Italy, Petrofina of Belgium, and the Petronord Group of seven French companies and one from Norway. The Ekofisk oil field is 185 miles (298 km) from Norway and 200 miles (320 km) from Scotland.

6 | Two masterpiece paintings, Paul Gauguin's "A Still Life of Apples and Grapes" and Pierre Bonnard's Les Deux Sauteuils ("The Two Chairs"), were stolen from the North London home of a British philanthropist Mathilda Marks-Kennedy, Sir Mark Kennedy, creating a mystery that would remain unsolved for the next 43 years. Sold for US$25 at a police auction in Turin in 1975 after being abandoned by the burglars in a railway station, the paintings would be found in 2014 in the home of an Italian auto worker who was unaware of their value. In 1970, the Gauguin was valued at £120,000 (US$228,000) and the Bonnard at £35,000 (US$84,000). By 2014, the worth of the Gauguin and the Bonnard works together would be valued at US$50,000,000. The good faith purchaser "known only as Nicolo", would be allowed to keep the Gauguin painting.

13 | "The Long and Winding Road" became the Beatles' 20th and final single to reach number one on the U.S. Billboard Hot 100 chart in the magazine's June 13 rankings. Billboard's magazine and Top 40 had been released on June 6 . The song would stay a second week at #1 before dropping to #4 and moving back down the charts. During their six-year recording career, the Beatles had averaged one number 1 hit single every 3.7 months.

18 | In a surprise upset, voters in the United Kingdom gave the UK's Edward Heath and the Conservative Party a majority in the House of Commons, ending the leadership of the government by Prime Minister Harold Wilson and the rule by the Labor Party after nearly six years. Most opinion polls had predicted a third successive Labor win. The Labor Party had been so heavily favored that British bookmakers had set odds of 7 to 2 against the Conservatives winning control of Commons. The Tories won 330 of the 630 seats in the Commons, gaining 77 while Labor lost 75 to win only 288 seats. Before the election, Labor had a 364 to 253 majority.

21 | Brazil defeated Italy, 4–1, to win the 1970 FIFA World Cup before a crowd of 112,000 in Mexico City's Azteca Stadium. Both nations' teams had won the World Cup twice— Brazil in 1958 and 1962, and Italy in 1934 and 1938, so the Jules Rimet Trophy, to be awarded permanently to the first three-time winner, was at stake.

23 | Prince Charles, heir apparent to the throne of the United Kingdom, received a Bachelor of Arts degree from Trinity College, Cambridge, becoming the first future British monarch to obtain a college diploma . The heir to the throne had been criticized as being unqualified to be accepted into Cambridge University, an institution with the highest academic standards, and surprised his detractors by earning a second-class division one degree.

24 | The first videodisc, the Television Electronic Disc (TeD), was demonstrated at a press conference in West Berlin by Teldec, a joint venture of the West German electronics manufacturer AEG Telefunken and Britain's Decca Records . The 20 centimeters (7.9 in) flexible foil disc was capable of storing roughly five minutes of video programming, and would be upgraded to longer times by the time it went on sale on March 17, 1975.

25 | Construction began on the first high-speed rail system in Europe, the Firenze—Roma direttisima. The 254 kilometers (158 mi) line would open on February 24, 1977.

2 | Conservative Party rule began in the House of Commons after Queen Elizabeth II addressed the Commons and the House of Lords for the traditional State Opening of Parliament. The Queen spoke on the plans of Edward Heath's government for reducing taxes, reforming relations between management and labor, curbing immigration and reducing the government's intervention in business affairs. Prime Minister Heath then addressed the Commons and said that he planned to lift the ban on the sale of weapons to South Africa.

3 | All 112 persons aboard Dan-Air Flight 1903 were killed when the airliner crashed into the sea on its approach to Barcelona. The De Havilland Comet had been chartered to take 105 passengers from northern England to Spain for a 13-day holiday vacation, and had departed Manchester earlier.

10 | Bishop James Edward Walsh was allowed to leave the People's Republic of China after 12 years imprisonment, and walked across a footbridge into Hong Kong. Walsh, a Roman Catholic priest, had been arrested in 1958 and sentenced to 20 years imprisonment. In a statement, the PRC's Xinhua News Agency said that Walsh had been released because of "old age and ill health" and added that "the culprit confessed his crimes while serving his term". Walsh said that the Chinese had been "very polite" to him during his dozen years imprisonment, and that he had been incarcerated with two English-speaking inmates.

13 | "Orange Day" parades, organized by Northern Ireland's Protestant Orange Order took place peacefully in Belfast and in 18 other towns in the United Kingdom's six Northern Ireland counties, with 100,000 participants. The Belfast event attracted 40,000 marchers demonstrating in favor of keeping predominantly Protestant Northern Ireland separate from the mostly Catholic Republic of Ireland. A security force of 20,000 British Army troops and local police maintained order, and only three arrests of Catholic opponents were reported. The celebrations, normally held on July 12 to commemorate the 1690 Battle of the Boyne, were postponed one day because the 12th fell on a Sunday.

15 | The United Kingdom's 47,000 longshoremen walked out on strike at the end of the day shift, tying up Great Britain's 40 major ports for the first time since 1926. Queen Elizabeth II proclaimed a state of emergency the next morning as dockworkers refused to load or unload nearly 100 ships already in harbor. The longshoremen returned to work on August 3 after delegates of the Transport and General Workers Union voted on July 29 to accept a compromise brokered by a court of inquiry, approving it 51 to 31.

July

20 | Iain Macleod, the British Chancellor of the Exchequer and second only to Prime Minister Edward Heath in the new Conservative Party government, died suddenly at the age of 56 after only one month in office. Macleod had served for only 18 days before being hospitalized on July 8 for an emergency appendectomy, almost immediately after making a speech during the opening of Parliament. He had discharged only a day before a fatal heart attack, which took place without warning at the Chancellor's official residence at 11 Downing Street in London.

21 | The Aswan High Dam in Egypt was completed after a decade of work and one billion dollars in aid from the Soviet Union The engineers completed the Aswan Dam in southern Egypt. The damming of the Nile River created Lake Nasser, requiring the relocation of 50,000 residents of Egypt and Sudan and placing unexcavated archaeological sites underwater. Before the flooding, the Egyptian government had relocated the statue of Pharaoh Ramses II at Abu Simbel to higher ground. The hydroelectric dam provides electricity and now protects farmers in the Nile Valley from floods and from the effects of drought.

25 | New Zealand's rugby union team, which had not lost a game in the past five years, was defeated by the second most successful team in the world, South Africa's Springboks, in a match before 55,000 spectators in Pretoria. The "All Blacks" of New Zealand had won 17 consecutive international matches and 55 in a row at home against domestic competition, but were behind, 12 to 0, at the end of the first half and went on to lose the match, 17 to 6.

29 | British longshoremen ended their strike that had tied up the nation's ports for most of the month. Delegates to the Transport and General Workers Union voted, 51 to 31, to accept Lord Pearson's plan for management to increase its guaranteed minimum pay from £16 to £20 (US$38.40 to $48) per week.

31 | After 238 years, the traditional daily drink of rum for British sailors was ended as the Royal Navy ended the rum ration — the "tot" that had been permitted for British seamen since 1731 . The Navy had announced its plan to end the daily serving of 95.5 proof rum a year earlier, concluding (as one report described it) that "rum-soaked sailors had no place in a modern warship". While the serving of rum would still be permitted for special occasions, the daily issue of rum (for 39,000 sailors in 130 ships and frigates) was ended.

August

2 | Rubber bullets, designed by the UK's Ministry of Defense as a non-lethal method of riot control, were used for the first time. The "L2A2", made of hard rubber, was first employed by the British Army against protesters in Northern Ireland, particularly children. Because they were "highly inaccurate", the bullets were fired into crowds, often by "skip firing" to bounce the projectiles off of the ground and into groups. Although the intent was to cause pain without killing or maiming an individual, the bullets caused numerous serious injuries and several deaths; over 55,000 would be fired during the Northern Ireland conflict until being discontinued at the end of 1974.

9 | A head-on collision between two trains killed 33 people and injured at least 136 south of the resort town of Plentzia in Spain's Basque region. A southbound train had pulled out from Plentzia with vacationing families and weekend visitors from the seaside of the Bay of Biscay and returning to Bilbao. Employees of the railway station at Urduliz had signaled for an empty train to depart the station on a northbound trip to pick up more passengers from Plentzia.

12	Two French soccer football teams, Stade Saint-Germain and Paris Football Club, completed their merger to begin play as Paris Saint-Germain F.C. (PSG), which would become one of the most successful professional teams in France. PSG won the Division 2 title in the 1970-71 season and was promoted to France's premier circuit, Ligue 1, where it has won eight titles and been the champion for five consecutive seasons, as well as 12 Coupe de France and eight Coupe de la Ligue championships.
15	The 1970-1971 professional soccer football seasons opened for The Football League's four divisions and 92 teams in England. The new season featured three innovations in the form of corporate-sponsored promotional events, with the preseason Watney Mann Invitation Cup (an eight team playoff between the top goal scoring teams in each of the divisions); the Texaco Cup (an 18-team competition among First Division teams in the UK's four leagues, with six English playing six Scottish teams and two Northern Irish playing two Welsh teams in the opening round), and the Ford Sporting League, which was a prize given monthly to a team under a scoring system that awarded points for goals scored and subtracted points for players being penalized.
19	Britain's second Skynet communications satellite was launched from Cape Kennedy in the United States, following up on the November launch of the first Skynet. The intent was to park Skynet 1A in a geo-stationary orbit outpost over the Indian Ocean to aid communications from Britain to military outposts in Asia and Africa. Unfortunately, when the second Skynet was being raised toward its permanent site on August 22, its motor ceased firing halfway through its 27 second sequence and the satellite was lost

22	Panama resumed control of a U.S. Army base at Rio Hato, after declining to renew a 15-year agreement to lease the property to the United States. The 29 square miles (75 km2) base, which was converted into a civilian airport, had served as the training site for the 193rd Infantry Brigade since 1962.

August

26 In one of the worst U.S. aircraft losses in the Vietnam War, 32 U.S. servicemen were killed when a rocket-propelled grenade struck a U.S. Army CH-47 Chinook helicopter as the transport was preparing to land at Firebase Judy in South Vietnam's Quang Nam Province. The Chinook was carrying 25 American troops, and debris struck seven others on the ground.

30 The third, and last, annual Isle of Wight Festival ended after three days of rock, pop and jazz performances before a crowd that reached 250,000 people, most of whom were able to get in without paying or who watched from a hillside. Headlined by Joan Baez, the list of stars included Jimi Hendrix (in one of his last appearances), The Who, Joni Mitchell, The Doors, Emerson, Lake & Palmer, The Moody Blues, Chicago, Jethro Tull, Miles Davis, Tiny Tim and Leonard Cohen. The festival took place near Freshwater on Britain's Isle of Wight and was marked by drug arrests, minor riots, and financial losses for the producers, Fiery Creations, Ltd.

September

1 An assassination attempt against King Hussein of Jordan precipitates the Black September crisis.

5 Formula One driver Jochen Rindt is killed in qualifying for the Italian Grand Prix. He becomes World Driving Champion anyhow, first to earn the honor posthumously.

6 In September 6, 1970, members of the Popular Front for the Liberation of Palestine (PFLP) hijacked four airliners bound for New York City and one for London. Three aircraft were forced to land at Dawson's Field, a remote desert airstrip near Zarqa, Jordan, formerly Royal Air Force Station Zerqa, which then became PFLP's 'Revolutionary Airport'. By the end of the incident, one hijacker had been killed and one injury reported. This was the second instance of mass aircraft hijacking, after an escape from communist Czechoslovakia in 1950.

10 Elvis Presley begins his first concert tour since 1958 in Phoenix, Arizona, at the Veterans Memorial Coliseum.

15 King Hussein of Jordan forms a military government with Muhammad Daoud as the prime minister.

17 "Black September": King Hussein of Jordan orders the Jordanian Armed Forces to oust Palestinian fedayeen from Jordan.

29 In Berlin, Red Army Faction members rob three banks, with loot totaling over DM200,000.

October

2 | Pink Floyd releases Atom Heart Mother. It becomes their first number one album.

5 | The Front de libération du Québec (FLQ) kidnaps James Cross in Montreal and demands release of all its imprisoned members. The next day the Canadian government announces it will not meet the demand, beginning Quebec's October Crisis.

8 | Vietnam War: In Paris, a Communist delegation rejects U.S. President Richard Nixon's October 7 peace proposal as "a maneuver to deceive world opinion."

10 | October Crisis: In Montreal, a national crisis hits Canada when Quebec Minister of Labor Pierre Laporte becomes the second statesman kidnapped by members of the FLQ terrorist group.

15 | A section of the new West Gate Bridge in Melbourne collapses into the river below, killing 35 construction workers.

17 | October Crisis: Pierre Laporte is found murdered in south Montreal.

22 | Chilean army commander René Schneider is shot in Santiago; the government declares a state of emergency. Schneider dies October 25.

28 | A cholera outbreak in eastern Slovakia causes Hungary to close its border with Czechoslovakia.

30 | In Vietnam, the worst monsoon to hit the area in six years causes large floods, kills 293, leaves 200,000 homeless and virtually halts the Vietnam War.

November

1 The Club Cinq-Sept fire was a major blaze at a nightclub just outside Saint-Laurent-du-Pont, Isère in south-eastern France on Sunday, 1 November 1970. The catastrophe claimed the lives of 146 people, almost all of whom were aged between 17 and 30. The scale of the disaster shocked the French nation. Subsequent official enquiries revealed a catalogue of shortcomings, oversights and evasions with regard to fire safety at both local and department level. Criminal charges were brought against a number of people; some received suspended jail sentences.

5 Vietnam War: The United States Military Assistance Command in Vietnam reports the lowest weekly American soldier death toll in five years (24 soldiers die that week, which is the fifth consecutive week the death toll is below 50; 431 are reported wounded that week, however).

8 The British comedy television series, The Goodies debuts on BBC Two.

10 Vietnam War – Vietnamization: For the first time in five years, an entire week ends with no reports of United States combat fatalities in Southeast Asia.

13 1970 Bhola cyclone: A 120-mph (193 km/h) tropical cyclone hits the densely populated Ganges Delta region of East Pakistan (now Bangladesh), killing an estimated 500,000 people (considered the 20th century's worst cyclone disaster). It gives rise to the temporary island of New Moore / South Talpatti.

17 Luna programme: The Soviet Union lands Lunokhod 1 on Mare Imbrium (Sea of Rains) on the Moon. This is the first roving remote-controlled robot to land on another world, and is released by the orbiting Luna 17 spacecraft.

20 The Miss World 1970 beauty pageant, hosted by Bob Hope at the Royal Albert Hall, London is disrupted by Women's Liberation protesters. Earlier on the same evening a bomb is placed under a BBC outside broadcast vehicle by The Angry Brigade, in protest at the entry of separate black and white contestants by South Africa.

23 Rodgers and Hammerstein's Oklahoma! Makes its network TV debut, when CBS telecasts the 1955 film version as a three-hour Thanksgiving special.

December

3 | October Crisis: In Montreal, kidnapped British Trade Commissioner James Cross is released by the Front de libération du Québec terrorist group after being held hostage for 60 days. Police negotiate his release and in return the Government of Canada grants 5 terrorists from the FLQ's Chenier Cell their request for safe passage to Cuba.

7 | Giovanni Enrico Bucher, the Swiss ambassador to Brazil, is kidnapped in Rio de Janeiro; kidnappers demand the release of 70 political prisoners.

13 | The government of Poland announces food price increases. Riots and looting lead to a bloody confrontation between the rioters and the government on December 15.

15 | The USSR's Venera 7 becomes the first spacecraft to land successfully on Venus and transmit data back to Earth.

17 | Polish 1970 protests: Soldiers fire on civilians returning to work in Gdynia. Martial law is imposed in the country until December 22.

20 | An Egyptian delegation leaves for Moscow to ask for economic and military aid.

23 | The North Tower of the World Trade Center in New York City is topped out at 1,368 feet (417 m), making it the tallest building in the world.

28 | The suspected killers of Pierre Laporte, Jacques and Paul Rose and Francis Sunard, are arrested near Montreal.

30 | In Viscaya in the Basque country of Spain, 15,000 go on strike in protest at the Burgos trial death sentences. Francisco Franco commutes the sentences to 30 years in prison.

31 | Paul McCartney sues in Britain to dissolve The Beatles' legal partnership.

The Year You Were Born 1970
Book by Sapphire Publishing

Made in the USA
Columbia, SC
01 May 2020